**Michael Carlson**

Th[e]

# OLIV[ER] [ST]ONE

www.pocketessentials.com

First published in Great Britain 2002 by Pocket Essentials, 18 Coleswood Road, Harpenden, Herts, AL5 1EQ

Distributed in the USA by Trafalgar Square Publishing, PO Box 257, Howe Hill Road, North Pomfret, Vermont 05053

Copyright © Michael Carlson 2002
Series Editor: Steve Holland

A CIP catalogue record for this book is available from the British Library.

ISBN 1-903047-92-7

2 4 6 8 10 9 7 5 3 1

Book typeset by Wordsmith Solutions Ltd
Printed and bound by Cox & Wyman

*This one, so much about fathers and sons, is for my father,*
*Roy O Carlson*
*(1926-1996)*
*who went with me to see JFK and decided Oswald acted alone*

## Acknowledgements

Thanks, and a tip of the aircraft carrier baseball cap with scrambled egg on the brim to Michael Goldfarb, Steven Kallaugher, Jeanine Basinger, Jude Schneider, Michael Connelly, Steve Holland, Kirsten Ellis, Tom Bogdanowicz, Barry Forshaw, Tertia Goodwin, Mark Webster, George Pelecanos and, as usual, Ion Mills.

# CONTENTS

# 1: Introduction: Conflict And Contradiction

Oliver Stone's film career throws up immense paradoxes. He approaches big issues as a pulp-fiction guy, brings a kinetic sense of visuals to documentary style material and follows the rules of melodrama even as he inserts pulp metaphysics into his stories. His films mix a fiercely moral overview with indulgence, excess and sleaze. As a result, few directors are simultaneously so idolised and reviled.

His admirers see him as a crusading voice of courage almost uniquely committed to a cinema engaged with political issues. He is admired as a daring craftsman whose visuals entice and whose experiments with editing and formats break new ground and allow him to make entertainment out of ideas.

He is also seen as a crackpot polemicist, an exploiter of sleaze, a male-oriented director unable to avoid objectifying women even in films about them. He is criticised as ham-fisted, loading pretentious visuals with obvious correlatives to the story and playing tricks with editing and technology simply to stay ahead of the cutting edge of pop videos. He is known for creating tension and conflict on his sets, yet he has also elicited some of the great performances of the past two decades, as well as surprising turns from character actors and a number of fine early performances from people who went on to greater things. Anthony Hopkins called him "the best director I ever worked with…he's a loose cannon like Orson Welles—he's daring."

Stone's image in the popular imagination as a controversial conspiracy nut has become so automatic a response that he even played himself in the Presidential comedy *Dave*, appearing on CNN as the only person in America who believed (correctly, of course) that Kevin Kline was actually an impostor. American network news regularly uses his name to deride any suggestion of conspiracy or double-dealing by the political establishment.

But the man who courts controversy has also been at the forefront of Hollywood's conscience. Stone harks back to an earlier era when Hollywood was enraptured by what David Thomson described as its belief "it can turn complex ideas and problems into crowd-pleasing movies." Films today have abdicated much of that function, leaving it to made-for-TV movies, but Stone has kept it alive. His films are 'big' in the sense that they attack issues—and Stone is adept at catching the crest of an issue's wave.

*Salvador* anticipated America's awareness of the depth and viciousness of Reaganite unlawfulness in Central America; *Wall Street*'s release appeared to be synchronised to the market's crash; the shock jocks of *Talk Radio* now hold court on American network news programmes; even *Natu-*

*ral Born Killers* could not have imagined tabloid TV bottom-feeder Geraldo Rivera grabbing a pistol and heading off to Afghanistan to personally kick some Talibutt.

The phrase "Oliver Stone's America" has been used frequently by critics analysing Stone's work but the equation might better be inverted, to see Stone as very much a quintessentially American artist, America's Oliver Stone. He is a cinematic version of the young Thomas Wolfe, a comparison intensified by the 1997 publication of his early novel *A Child's Night Dream*. His early scripts grew out of his ambitions as a young novelist, full of the sort of bubbling energy and intellectual Manifest Destiny which assumes the world is out there to be analysed, understood and conquered, and the defining sense that once you've been to Vietnam you can never go home again.

Stone is a child of the privileged 1950s America. But, unlike most young Americans in his position, he experienced the Vietnam War from the inside. If Vietnam shattered the idealistic Fifties view of America held by many who grew up then, it did so even more crushingly for those who fought there. Many of Stone's films have been criticised for eulogising a lost American innocence on the grounds that, as James Ellroy put it, "America was never innocent. We popped our cherry on the boat over and never looked back." The point is not that America was innocent, but that Americans believed they were, and, in Stone's youth, had that belief shattered forcibly by events.

So Stone's work is often informed by a moral sense which, in its typically American disdain of grey areas, can be traced straight back to the Protestant ethic within which America has always wrapped the bad with the good. These were the values implanted in him by his Jewish stockbroker father. But they often conflict with a prodigious self-indulgence, which may reflect his more indulgent, hedonistic French Catholic mother. The synthesis of Stone's values was forged by surviving the random chaos of war and having his eyes opened by drugs and popular, as opposed to elite, culture. He has insisted on indulging such pleasures fearlessly in his films, which often leaves them open to charges of pretentiousness and excess.

Yet his movies are also films about ideas which reflects a particularly Puritan sense of art's utilitarianism. Kevin Costner's rigid and moral Jim Garrison in *JFK* may be Stone's most revealing hero.

Like his heroes, Stone seeks enlightenment and, like them, what he finds and generates is conflict. He is the ultimate disillusioned idealist, discovering so many injustices about which he can be indignant. The result of this soul-searching is that all Stone's heroes must come to recognise the presence of the beast within themselves. That beast manifests itself literally in

8

his two horror movies and makes its literal return in *Natural Born Killers*, described perceptively by Stephen Schiff as "a penny dreadful blown up into an act of outrage." Significantly, *Natural Born Killers* may have been the first time Stone misjudged his ability to present ideas in a way the Hollywood community could not at least admire.

Because admire him they do. Stone has collected Oscar nominations and awards for impressing Hollywood with meaningful themes. The Academy has always loved to reward liberal films made with very conservative approaches and Stone's films have always been carefully balanced to avoid radicalism, even though that balance is often missed by critics. Underneath the politics, his films are deeply rooted in personal conflict, and Americans prefer to see issues in terms of personal trials and rugged individualism.

Stone's political conflicts are resolved in the personal sphere and for personal reasons: in *Wall Street* Bud Fox doesn't decide greed is bad, he gets offended because Gordon Gekko double-crosses him and breaks the promises he made to his father. *JFK* never solves the question of who killed Kennedy but Jim Garrison's family comes to forgive him his obsession.

Stone gets harsher criticism when he posits larger forces at work. Ironically *JFK* was attacked from the right for suggesting conspiracies and from the left for suggesting John Kennedy was a force for liberal change. But Stone's films are not only anchored in the struggles of individuals searching for salvation, meaning or simply peace. They focus their issues within a framework borrowed from the cinema of exploitation. Rapes figure largely as motivation in both *Salvador* and *Heaven And Earth*; Mallory's key sex scene in *Natural Born Killers* is an inverted rape scene as well. Stone always pulls at least one element of genre to the fore in every movie. He began directing horror films and writing violent genre movies and those footprints remain in almost all his work. *JFK* is at heart a film noir, a paranoid version of the pseudo-documentary crime films—say, *The Phenix City Story*—with the documentary footage echoing the pilgrim's progress of a DA, naïve to a credibility-stretching degree, who uncovers an evil underworld where white is black, black is white and little is grey. *Platoon*, of course, is a combat film, but so too are *Salvador*, *Born On The Fourth Of July* and *Heaven And Earth*. Those genre footprints reflect Stone's rich background in cinema, first as a film student at NYU and then as a screenwriter working on genre flicks while writing the historical dramas he hoped to direct.

# 2: Rosetta Stones: Cinematic Contexts

Thinking of Stone as a modern day Stanley Kramer isn't quite accurate. Though his films contain messages and his stories have a moral for the audience to take home, imagine Kramer's movies directed by Martin Scorsese and you'll get a better idea of Stone's cinema. It's no coincidence that the truest adaptation of a Stone screenplay came from the ultimate director of style for its own sake, Brian De Palma. Like Scorsese's films, Stone's are fiercely manipulative, but where Scorsese celebrates film style above all else and goes for the audiences' emotions, Stone wants to manipulate the audiences' minds as well as their hearts. Hence his constant reliance on what we will call 'The Thumper'—the point in his films where he calls 'time out', turns to the audience and explains the moral of the story as if he were afraid they had missed it.

These Western Union moments may indicate a fear that he has buried his points underneath the veneer of entertainment, although that would require him to be far more subtle than he has ever tried to be. Yet his ability to bring together visual style, personal conflict and the tools of exploitation helps him redirect much of the self-conscious self-importance of a Kramer. The films are just as commercial but less crass.

It is also no coincidence, and just as telling, that Stone's first big break came from screenwriter Robert Bolt, creator of historical epics like *Lawrence Of Arabia* and *A Man For All Seasons*, who must be counted a major influence. You can see from Bolt's films how Stone learned to find personal conflicts which could dramatise larger issues on a more accessible level.

Another strong influence on Stone were the directors he often cites as his film-school idols and his major inspirations: Orson Welles, Luis Buñuel and the French New Wave, particularly Alain Resnais and Jean-Luc Godard. The New Wave is the common ground of Stone and Scorsese: the excitement of shooting hand-held, trying different formats, the willingness to let the camera be an actor in the film and let the audience remain aware of its presence in every scene. Are the seeming excesses of *Natural Born Killers* or the documentary and lecture style expositions of *JFK* really that far removed from Godard at his most didactic? We can also see the influence of Buñuel in Stone's indulgence in scenes that move close to dreams and fantasy and his willingness to pursue symbolism. Stone is rarely naturalistic, yet he is extremely successful at reproducing natural effects. He is adept at using flashy technique, without calling attention to it, for a specific sense of realism. Think of his fondness for swish-pans, as in the tense elevator scene between Bud Fox and his father in *Wall Street*. Rarely has the feeling of being swept up in an argument until you say things you don't want to say been better expressed.

Stone's reliance on thumpers may also be a reflection of another telling influence, one overlooked in studies of his work, namely Paddy Chayevsky. Chayevsky provides a link between Stone and the radical polemics of Group Theatre and the idealism of Stone's father's generation and the disillusionment of Stone and his generation.

Chayevsky's screenplay for *Marty* (1955) took those hopes and gave them the dramatic tensions of a love story just as everything became possible for working people in the Fifties. From that starting point of optimism, Chayevsky's work grew steadily bleaker. He wrote arguably the greatest satire of the Sixties (*The Americanization Of Emily*, 1964), followed by two films, *The Hospital* (1971) and *Network* (1976), which caught the crest of the change in American values engendered by the Sixties. Sound familiar? What is *Natural Born Killers* if not *Network* fused with Quentin Tarantino's version of *Badlands* or *Gun Crazy*? For that matter, Ron Kovic in *Born On The Fourth Of July* could be seen as Marty deprived of the possibility of finding a love-making partner.

The idealism of *The Hospital*'s George C Scott and *Network*'s Peter Finch becomes paranoid in the former and manic in the latter, and self-destructive in both cases. Stone's leading men start out either manic or paranoid or are forced that way by a demanding world. They must resist their self-destructiveness in order to survive, if not master, that world.

These issues highlight the comparison between Stone and the film-makers he most resembles stylistically: Fifties icons Samuel Fuller and, especially, Robert Aldrich. Like Fuller, Stone's experience as a combat infantryman informs all his work; Vietnam remains the defining event of Stone's life. The paradox that he didn't need to fight as a private in that war but chose to do so is a foreshadowing of almost all the choices he made through his career. It also separates him from most of Hollywood, where the newer generations' aesthetic sensibilities come from watching films and not from experience.

Fuller was always willing to let the camera stand in for his own perception, to put his audience directly into his own reaction, to shove life in their faces. If Fuller's films are collections of tabloid headlines that scream for your attention, Aldrich's are often seen as purer sensationalism, yet underneath them is a liberal sensibility not that far removed from Stanley Kramer's. Sometimes it seems as if Stone has set out to remake the entire Aldrich oeuvre. Boyle and Doc Rock descend on Salvador like the mercenaries of *Vera Cruz* on Mexico; *Platoon* recalls *Attack* in many ways; and if

11

Sergeant Barnes and his rednecks aren't a direct descendant of Lee Marvin's civilian-killing *Dirty Dozen* what are they? Of course *Any Given Sunday* recalls *The Longest Yard* while Sean Penn's male bimbo in *U Turn* echoes Burt Reynolds in *Hustle.* When he makes a picture specifically about women, Stone's *Heaven And Earth* sometimes seems as depressing as *The Killing Of Sister George.*

The mix of influences seen in Stone's work is an uneasy one, as if Fuller, Aldrich, Scorsese and the New Wave battle on one side against Chayevsky, Bolt and Warren Beatty's *Reds* on the other. But there is one other filmmaker with whom a revealing comparison can be made, one who helps us in considering how Stone draws those two strands together in his work. Anthony Hopkins' comparison of Stone to Orson Welles is not as far-fetched as it might seem on the surface.

Andrew Sarris' thumbnail description of Welles as an "ageing enfant terrible" certainly fits Stone better than any other contemporary director, with less emphasis on the 'ageing', perhaps, and more on the 'terrible'. In the sense that Sarris implied a spoiled brat at work, like Mozart in *Amadeus*, it was better—in fact coldly—suited to Welles. Yet if one were searching for a single word to describe Stone's work, the best might be 'excess', with all its negative connotations. Stone is driven to stretch boundaries to their limits: artistic, personal, psychological. Thus the hallmarks of his career can be seen as indulgence as much as invention. An ability, indeed a desire, to shock as much as a talent for telling powerful stories. Much the same could be said about Welles, even in his days in theatre and radio.

The most vivid surface similarity is, of course, the way each director's best-known film was the subject of intense efforts to censor or stop it before its release and of severe criticism—often from those outside the usual critical circles—immediately afterward. That *Citizen Kane* was Welles' first film appeared to produce in him a wariness that resulted in his running out on his other great studio films before he could be involved in the process of their diminishment. In Stone's case, the controversy over the reaction to *JFK,* if anything, contributed to the immense box-office success of the film and his willingness to court controversy is something of a function of the control he retains over his output.

Gary Wills makes a persuasive argument that *Nixon*, not *JFK,* is Stone's *Kane*, what he calls the attempt to "fathom the mystery of a mystery-less man." Both are stories of boys cut off from parental love who replace love with great ambition and drive. One can easily fit both Stone's and Welles' upbringings into a similar framework. Such relations lie at the heart of Welles' first two films; they are reflected in almost all of Stone's. Both men were, to some extent, autodidactics; Welles' education coming in theatre and radio, with his trip to Ireland perhaps the equivalent of Stone's reinvention of himself on the battlefields of Vietnam. Like Welles, Stone drew on some superb technical allies in order to use the language of film for his own purposes and he has been willing to experiment with vision and sound to achieve effects that arise out of other media (in Welles' case from theatre and radio, in Stone's from writing and reportage).

Stone isn't the next Orson Welles. Even where their searching for visual correlatives to narrative emotions of their stories seems similar, Welles was subtle, where Stone is, shall we say, less so. The difference in their relationship to 'Hollywood' (however we define the film business) is instructive too. Where for years Welles struggled to get the wherewithal to make movies, Stone has become in many ways a consummate insider. Stone has allied himself with independent money-men, some of whom, like John Daly and Arnon Milchan, are legendary operators, and has survived, indeed, prospered with them. And where Welles was idolised without ever being accepted into or honoured by the Hollywood community, Stone has been Hollywood's favourite kind of troublemaker, the kind whose films make money. Tellingly, his most controversial films have done best at the box office.

Stone has used his success to set up a production company which, far from being restricted to Oliver Stone films, has been far more of a mini-studio in the traditional sense of facilitating other people's projects. That conflict, between critic of the system and player within, is a reflection of all Stone's other dichotomies: the clash of influences, personal and cinematic; the conflict between high-minded moralising and the reliance on shock and exploitation. The contradictions in Stone's personae as critic of the system and player within it reflect a similar conflict in his film-making.

# 3: Let's Go Get Stoned: A Cinema Of Excess

Drugs have certainly influenced the making of many Hollywood films but Stone, who turned away from cocaine before most of Hollywood, may be the first director whose films continue to reflect the experience of mind-expanding drugs as part of their aesthetic. In most of his films, the pacing, the characters' behaviour and the visual sense reflect the drugs the characters are taking or, in some cases, ought to be taking. All Stone's films need to be viewed from the protagonists' point of view; he's careful to keep its integrity and it's often interpreted as being his own. But as befits a filmmaker whose work is grounded in conflict and contradiction, all Stone's films pose crucial decisions for their protagonists.

*Characters & Choices*: Most of Stone's characters are conflicted. All face disillusionment. They are idealists, bruised by a reality that doesn't live up to their expectations. To cope with the loss of their illusions they are forced to become obsessed. Some, like Richard Boyle, start that way. Others, like Bud Fox, discover it when they find their dreams are hollow. *Platoon*'s Chris Taylor, looking for enlightenment and a sense of meaning through war, is forced to choose between father figures. Ron Kovic, a true believer, finds his ideals as shattered as his body by the reality behind the Vietnam War and, by extension, America.

As suggested earlier, many of these choices have their roots in the contrast and conflict between Stone's own parents. Families occupy a strange place in Stone's films. They symbolise the safety of personal morality and the uselessness of such morality in the real world. Men need to choose between their own stability with the faithful, supportive woman who symbolises it and the path of their obsession, their career, and the women who come along with that. It is not always a literal Madonna/whore dilemma but it usually follows that paradigm. Characters without family attachments find substitutes to drive them onward. In this, Tony Montana and Richard Nixon bookend his cinema, asking the same question: can you sacrifice everything personally in order to conquer society? Willie Beamen in *Any Given Sunday* faces the same choice. As Bud Fox asks, "How much is enough?" The answer with obsessives is that there is never enough.

This sense of obsession may be part of Stone's success with actors. He gets great performances from established stars but also casts brilliantly, using young actors before they are known (Johnny Depp in *Platoon*), frequently casting against type (Michael Douglas in *Wall Street*) and assembling an effective, if changing, ensemble company of character performers.

But there are few such parts for actresses. Until Joan Chen's performance as Mama in *Heaven And Earth*, Cindy Gibb's small rôle as a raped and murdered lay worker in *Salvador* may have been his most complex female rôle. Since then, Joan Allen's brilliant performance in *Nixon* and Juliette Lewis' lead in *Natural Born Killers* could be added, but it remains a very short list. The absence of roles for women is one of the most distinctive of Stone's cinematic trademarks.

*Stone Killers—Women*: Stone often attributes his attitude toward women as being developed in his all-male upbringing of private schools and the army. He says his first serious experiences were with whores while teaching in Vietnam. It could be argued that the recurring dilemma of the woman as a threat to a man's creative drive goes back to his parents: Stone's mother (who always called him Oliver, which is actually his middle name) represented both an alternative to his father's work ethic (and repressed poetical drives) and a lascivious erotic dead-end (which formed the subject of his early screenplay *Dominique* and received an incestuous airing in his novel).

Since his films are almost exclusively about the choices forced on men to be men, women often symbolise the conflict between creative and destructive energies. In his first film, *Seizure*, Nicole sacrifices herself to save her child and the writer/hero; in *Midnight Express*, Billy's reaction to his girlfriend's visit is to masturbate while she exposes her breasts. Many women exist simply to divert the hero from the course he must pursue. Some (Darryl Hannah in *Wall Street,* Meg Foster in *Born On The Fourth Of July*) fall by the wayside; others (Sissy Spacek in *JFK*, Joan Allen in *Nixon)* see the light and stand by their man.

Even when Stone builds a film around a woman *(Heaven And Earth)*, he concentrates on her abuse and humiliation rather than her triumph. Although the essence of the film is Le Ly's liberation, what we see is a catalogue of her subservience in both her own and American culture. When she returns to Vietnam a success, Stone lets her brother and son undercut that success, as if redefining her subservience.

He also litters his films with eye candy, the kind of appearances that send the males in the audience scanning the credits to discover the likes of Andrea Thompson, Marlena Bielinska or Corinna Laszlo, ravished by the camera in bit parts. Mother figures are also problematic. They range from Puritanical figures like Le Ly's or Ron Kovic's mothers to ditzy playgirls like Ann Margaret in *Any Given Sunday* or Debbie Reynolds in *Heaven And Earth* but are more usually non-existent or nearly so (for example, the barely visible Millie Perkins in *Wall Street)*.

*Madonnas And Whores*: The choice is often disguised but still clear. In *Talk Radio*, Laura isn't a whore, just a girl looking to have a career, but we get the point. Le Ly's refusal to whore herself in *Heaven And Earth* seems crucial to Stone; when she finally gives in to the offer she can't refuse, you can almost sense a sort of Churchillian "we've established what you are, now we're just haggling over the price" satisfaction. Even lay worker Moore in *Salvador* flirts with Boyle in a bar just before she suffers her fate surrounded by gratuitous shots of rapists exposing nuns' breasts. Stone never did get to direct his screenplay of *Evita* but the results would have been interesting; he described her as being like Tony Montana: "courageous, feisty, double-crossing bitch, goddess, mother, saint…I think she's a great character."

*Clashing Symbols*: As well as genre elements, another of Stone's devices for drawing his films beyond their immediate setting is a penchant for the mythological which also reflects his grounding in literature and fondness for literary themes. His martyrs, like the Greek-named Elias, may be portrayed in embarrassingly blatant Christ symbolism (and check out how many characters in his early screenplays are called Chris) or they can be placed in Tony Montana's Oedipal dilemma of having to kill the symbolic father and marry the mother.

He's also willing to give symbols life. He even inserts death as a character in both *The Doors* and *Natural Born Killers*, as if he were an Ingmar Bergman for the Nineties. He's fond of such symbolic images, sometimes showing them as they appear in the conscious, subconscious or mind-altered states of his characters. Often these will be so brief as to suggest subliminal information at the edges of normal perception.

Fire is the most important of these: from the flames leaping from bombs in *Salvador* to the napalm engulfing the land in *Platoon*, flames have become ever more stylised in his films, to the point where they shoot up like the fires of hell throughout *Natural Born Killers*.

Indians, shamans and desert mysticism are also commonplace. After all, this is a guy who chartered a plane to go off for a peyote weekend in South Dakota and wrote it off to research for *The Doors*. Mickey and Mallory do almost the same thing in *Natural Born Killers*, for which Stone apparently scouted locations for Indian scenes that weren't in the script ("there's always an Indian in my movies"). Sean Penn walks into a living peyote trip in *U Turn*, complete with flashes of what seems to be Jodorowsky's *El Topo* going through his head.

Of course, if you're tripping round the desert you ought to get to know your lizards. Lizards (and snakes) make regular appearances in Stone's films including, of course, the obvious ones: Jim Morrison, the Lizard King and Gordon Gekko, the gekko.

*Feel The Effect*: Stone likes to try to reproduce what his characters experience for the audience to share. At its simplest level, the story of *Scarface* moves at the pace and intensity of someone on a coke high all the way through, complete with the final burn-out. *The Doors* can be viewed as a complete LSD trip, filled with hallucinations, long periods of intense navel-regarding boredom and a reality let-down. Few directors have managed to convey the chaos and panic of battle as well as he does in *Platoon*, but think also of the different effect on the characters in the smaller battle scenes of, say, *Salvador* and *Heaven And Earth*. Within their intensity they tell us specific things about the outsiders caught up in the action. *Platoon* builds to the moment where Chris must release the beast inside him and we believe it when he does.

*Vietnam & Corporate America*: Just as Stone's life was defined by his two journeys to Vietnam and his experiences fighting there, so the war informs virtually all of his movies, even in the sense that *Natural Born Killer*'s violence can be read as the result of a violent media which lacks the reality of war as a counterweight to its sensationalism. Vietnam footage will play on TVs in the background of all Stone's period pieces; while we start to distrust Gordon Gekko when his use of Vietnam language and talk of war both ring flat.

The connection between the war and big-business' profit is made explicitly in *JFK* and his father's financial world will be a target from *Wall Street* onward, particularly in *Any Given Sunday*. In an interview, Stone talked about the way football had been ruined by the corporate interests whose commercial breaks slow the game down. As ever with Stone, his aversion is ambiguous. If you doubt that, try counting the number of Pepsi product placements. It marked a major coup when Dr Pepper appeared to have taken over as the pop drink of choice in *U Turn*.

*Stock Company & Film-Making Techniques*: Stone has not kept the sort of stock company together the way Clint Eastwood has at Malpaso but two of his relationships are crucial, particularly the partnership with cinematographer Robert Richardson. Richardson, with no feature film background, shot eleven consecutive movies in as many years with Stone, from *Platoon* to *U Turn*; this has to go down as one of the most successful partnerships between director and cinematographer in film history. Richardson brought documentary experience to the package which has been a major factor in all Stone's historical epics. Richardson has been willing to use multiple formats and seems adept at being able to anticipate what Stone will be looking for visually in order to illustrate his ideas. In general, the many-textured nature of the visuals helps accent specific images or ideas and amplify emotions. It is an instinctive grasp of Stone's nature of storytelling which appar-

17

ently survived years of high-energy bombast with only one serious bust-up. Richardson would eventually win a well-deserved Oscar for *JFK*.

Production designer Victor Kempster has been another Stone regular and the way the look of the films has changed over the years is a tribute to that relationship. The non-historical films of the Nineties are far more art-intensive, far more artificial in their look than those that preceded them. The increasing use of imagery in flash frames is a challenge to any designer.

Three of Stone's pictures have won Oscars for best editing, each time with a new team of young film editors. It might not be fair to attribute the eventual progression from Claire Simpson to David Brenner and Joe Hutshing to Hank Corwin to burn-out—and the progression is not a literal one anyway—but it is fair to say that Stone's idiosyncratic editing, his reliance on far more cutting that is usually considered necessary or reasonable, may be better suited to young and energetic editors.

Stone's music has been of inconsistent quality (indeed, Georges Delerue's score for *Salvador* strikes me as being as effective as his *Platoon* score is overdone). John Williams' typically dramatic score works better in *JFK* than in the more intensely personal focus of *Born On The Fourth Of July*. But increasingly, Stone has relied on existing music tracks, compiled with his music producer Budd Carr. In some cases, notably *The Doors* where the music is essential to the story, and *Natural Born Killers* where the tracks are integrated beautifully into the film, they have triumphed. In others, particularly *U Turn*, they are less successful. *U Turn*'s Ennio Morricone score often seems to conflict with the background music, sometimes getting lost in it.

Stone doesn't really have a stock company of actors but he has used some people repeatedly to good effect, ranging from the prototype Stone figures, James Woods and Tommie Lee Jones (who did four Stone films in succession), to the *tabula resa* that is Charlie Sheen. John C McGinley serves a Bruce Dern-like function for Stone. Tony Plana brings intensity to a number of rôles. Lesser known character actors like Frank Whaley, Michael Wincott or Mark Moses played crucial smaller rôles in a number of films, while Annie McEnroe and Dale Dye, the military advisor, turn up like good-luck charms.

*Creative Conflict*: The hilariously contradictory image of the Buddhist Stone terrorising the staff at his production company Ixtlan was the most memorable one in Stephen Schiff's 1994 *New Yorker* profile, but it has been a trademark of his mature career as a director. Robert Downey described the environment of *Natural Born Killers'* set as "Purgatory on a per-diem." His manipulating of collaborators is legendary: screenwriters he has barely met (he often prefers to work separately) will receive phone calls with severe criticism of their work. The roots of this, in military training where recruits are broken down and rebuilt, is obvious and it's no coincidence Stone famously sent his actors for basic training for *Platoon*.But it's also something that has always been part of the Hollywood mindgame, where power is accumulated and used in very precise ways. Stone has never shied away from his image of someone strewing conflict and controversy in his wake. Shying away is not his style. From the moment he impacted on Hollywood with his screenplay for *Midnight Express*, he has generated, if not courted, controversy.

# 4: Courting Controversy:
# Everybody Must Get Stoned

On 14 May 1991, a story by Jon Margolis appeared in Chicago Tribune syndication, including the *Dallas Morning News*. Headlined '*JFK* movie and book attempt to rewrite history', it reported the filming of Stone's *JFK*, characterising Stone as someone who "sees conspiracies everywhere," Jim Garrison (the film's lead character, on whose book the screenplay was in part based) as "bizarre," and predicted, since the film was financed by Time Warner, that *Time* magazine would promote it strongly. "There is a point at which intellectual myopia becomes morally repugnant," wrote Margolis. "Stone's new movie has passed that point...and so will anyone who pays American money to see the film."

Five days later, George Lardner Jr, the *Washington Post*'s writer on intelligence matters, followed up with a long story subtitled 'Dallas In Wonderland'. Working with a copy of the script's first draft leaked to him by assassination researcher Harold Weisberg, Lardner used Weisberg's disgruntled testimony to demolish many of Garrison's assassination theories and to characterise the entire operation as a group of madmen being orchestrated by Stone who was "in it to make a buck."

Criticism of a film, or its historical stance, is hardly unusual. Nor are attacks from the mainstream press on something they might believe is controversial. What made these attacks unique was that *JFK* had only just begun filming, under a blanket of supposed secrecy reminiscent of *Citizen Kane* at RKO (it was called 'Project X' by Stone's Ixtlan Films), and would not be released until 20 December. Yet, in the interim, the attacks intensified. In June *Time* ignored corporate synergy and weighed in, giving the lie to Margolis' assumptions. Robert Sam Anson, himself the author of an early compendium of JFK conspiracies, followed with a major feature in *Esquire*, which asked "Is he right? Does he care? Or is history just another Oliver Stone movie?"

As the release date neared, the major media's broadsides used their heaviest guns. The *New York Times* ran nearly thirty pieces, including a major pan by columnist Tom Wicker. The *Washington Post* dragged out George Will, as well as former President Gerald Ford (a Warren Commission member) and Commission counsel David Belin. *Newsweek* (given admiring reference in *Salvador*) ran a large piece called 'Twisted History', balanced by an appreciative review and interview by David Ansen. In a notable piece of dissent, the *Boston Globe*'s Washington columnist, Tom

Oliphant, wondered why his fellow political writers like Wicker and Will were so quick to condemn the film sight unseen.

Why Oliver Stone, and why *JFK*? The question is important because even though Stone had been no stranger to controversy in his career, nothing could have prepared him for this landslide of criticism.

Each of Stone's major screenplays had generated flak. With *Midnight Express* he was accused of denigrating the Turkish nation and—not for the last time—of homophobia. *Conan The Barbarian* was derided for its weapons-friendly fascism. *Scarface* was attacked for glamorising drugs and excessive violence as well as for being anti-Cuban. And *Year Of The Dragon* was charged with flaunting anti-Chinese racism and misogyny. Based on the reaction to Stone's screenplays, you might conclude he was a gun-loving, xenophobic, macho pig right-winger.

*Salvador* had changed that. Although Stone was careful to show balance (his rebels commit their own atrocities) his straightforward portrayal of the US government's covert involvement and the willingness of the intelligence community to subvert the US ambassador in anticipation of the upcoming Reagan reversal of US policy (a foreshadowing of one of Stone's major theses in *JFK*) made him a hero of sorts to the American left. He was credited for generating considerable support for those opposed to US policy in Central America.

His Vietnam movies struck a more positive chord in audiences, though *Platoon* was criticised for its portrayal of soldiers as drug-taking nihilists aware they were being sold out by profiteers and *Born On The Fourth Of July* for its condemnation of the Veteran's Administration and its seeming Democratic Party partisanship. The contradictions evident in *Wall Street* were enough to convince many that Stone was condemning capitalism where really his concerns were far more narrow and his judgement far more personal.

The opprobrium faced by *JFK* belied its popularity. Much of the venom can be explained by the way the film upstages mainstream journalists who for thirty years had failed to question the very obvious flaws in the Warren Report. Wicker, who wrote the *New York Times'* most virulent condemnation of the film, had authored the paper's front page response to the Warren Report the day after the 26 volumes were issued, announcing the case was closed. Investigation of the Kennedy assassination had for years been left to 'conspiracy buffs' whose findings could be dismissed along with UFO nuts. As Norman Mailer said, "journalists attack people who play games with fact because that's what they do, and they can't stand themselves."

*JFK* also drew fierce criticism because it suggested that American institutions were corrupt and that the corruption was symptomatic of the system.

The government itself was complicit in the assassination and the free press corrupt in its failure to pursue that angle. The attacks came from those most concerned with protecting their institutions.

There is always an element of distortion in fiction; both fiction and non-fiction require authorial choices. Certain elements of *JFK* took liberties, most notably in David Ferrie's confession to Garrison. Yet scenes attacked as being 'fiction' have since been shown to be true: Ferrie and Oswald were proven to have known each other and Clay Shaw's CIA affiliations were admitted. Stone came under great fire for his heroic portrayal of Garrison, yet argued convincingly that most of the 'character flaws' cited by the film's critics were part of an orchestrated smear campaign designed to discredit his case and never proven. Even a viciously anti-Garrison article in the *New York Times*, written well after the film's release by Warren apologist Gerald Posner, prompted a response from New Orleans citizens who knew Shaw as 'Clay Betrand', thus backing one of Garrison's main contentions.

*JFK* presented its case from the point of view of a lone crusader and presented alternate realities within that case. Its unequivocal point was that the Warren Report was wrong, the House Assassinations Committee's work had been left incomplete and the American people were no closer to the truth. And, because response to the film was responsible for the creation of the Assassination Records Review Board which released much material which was supposed to be withheld until we were all long dead, *JFK* can be judged as one of the most successful pieces of agitprop of all time. It reminds us of the famous dictum that if good art is art which does good, *Uncle Tom's Cabin* was the world's best novel.

Many viewers feel hectored by the film, as if Garrison were not giving them the chance to make up their own minds. Others sympathetic to conspiracy theories were offended by Stone's insistence that Kennedy was attempting a sea change in American policies. Some found the excesses of Shaw's gay masked ball gratuitous, echoing accusations that Garrison pursued Shaw because he was a homosexual. What was most impressive about the controversy was the way Stone was prepared to argue his case as a filmmaker not just with film critics but with journalists and historians. His annotated screenplay, published with a full record of the controversy, stands unique in film history. Stone has enjoyed his prominence as a political thinker, no matter how much he was derided, but the fact remains he had better things to do and the idea that he was committed enough to the ideas his film had raised to defend them for years afterward is impressive.

What's less impressive is the way that, despite the eventual justification of the film by time, he has become, literally, a symbol of political looniness in the American mainstream. The press always gets the last word. When Hilary Clinton suggested that the Whitewater, Paula Jones and Lewinsky affairs were being blown out of proportion to impeachment scale by a "vast right-wing conspiracy," the press immediately labelled her "an Oliver Stone" rather than examining the links between, say, Richard Mellon Scaife's 'Arkansas Project', Paula Jones' lawyers and Kenneth Starr. See how easy it is to sound like 'an Oliver Stone'?

The controversy surrounding *Natural Born Killers* was totally different but may have played on Stone's notoriety. *Natural Born Killers'* violence caused some furore, but the stylised nature of the film and its obvious aim to critique America's celebrity media rendered it, if anything, cartoony. Yet Stone, as ever, also indulged himself in the exploitative nature of the images, making it harder to position himself above the exploitation fray.

It became more difficult when Sarah Edmondson and Benjamin Darras, a pair of Louisiana 18-year-olds, went on a crime spree that included one murder and another victim left paralysed. Darras received a life sentence, Edmondson 35 years. They claimed to have been inspired by *Natural Born Killers* which they had watched after dropping acid—one of a string of similar disavowals of responsibility claimed by the lawyers of killers which range from the famous junk-food 'Twinkie' defence to blaming professional wrestling for deaths caused by kids imitating it.

Novelist John Grisham, a lawyer himself and a friend of the man murdered by the two, called publicly for film-makers to be held accountable for violence 'incited' by their work and a lawsuit was eventually filed against Stone and Warner Bros by the family of the second victim, in effect charging Stone's film with "product liability." The charges were originally dismissed, then reversed by an appellate court before Louisiana judge Robert Morrison finally ruled that the film was protected under First Amendment rights and that he saw no evidence its creators intended it to incite violence.

It was vindication for Stone but also served as a lesson of sorts about his films. Of course he can't be blamed when someone mistakes fiction for reality, but when you blur the line by trying to put the audience in the middle of your film it's not impossible for audiences to be captivated by the characters' glamour, especially when those characters become the objects of media adulation and frenzy. That the media and fans are being satirised is lost in the allure of the world Stone presents. After all, is Wayne Gale really any weirder than Ricki Lake? Are those fans really any dumber than a Jerry Springer audience? Is *Natural Born Killers'* satire not heavy-handed enough, or does the film celebrate, in true Stone fashion, that which it ostensibly condemns? Does form become substance rather than follow it? It is the question which Stone was building toward all his life.

# 5: Biography: Ollie Was A Rolling Stone

William Oliver Stone was born 15 September 1946 in New York City. His choice of name is significant because like many artists, often those from broken backgrounds, he has selected the most basic facet of his identity rather than simply accept the name given him. His father did the same: born Lou Silverstein into a wealthy New York garment family, he changed his name to Lou Stone when he attended Yale University which still operated under a strict quota system for Jews.

The Depression lowered the family's expectations. After Lou finished studying English at Yale he took a job as a department store floorwalker. Lou wrote poetry most of his life but never published it. Like so many others of his generation, a life changed by the Depression was changed even more by the war. As a colonel serving as a financial advisor on General Eisenhower's staff in Paris, he spotted a French woman riding past on a bicycle. He pursued, and eventually won, Jacqueline Goddard who came from a family of farmers. She came to America as a war bride and Lou Stone became successful on Wall Street as the publisher of an investment newsletter in which he indulged his dormant writing talents. Stone inevitably emphasises the dichotomies of his upbringing. His father worked tirelessly and had a hard attitude toward life, never appearing to feel content in himself—a sense his son attributes to the insecurity brought on by the memory of his grandfather's failure in the 1929 crash. He believed in hard work and certainly repressed his own creative impulses. In this he could be seen as the quintessential 1950s organisation man. His mother was far more lively, determined to enjoy life and the prosperity of the new world.

Stone received a privileged upbringing in Manhattan and the suburbs of Stamford, Connecticut. He went to Episcopal church, attended the posh Trinity School and spent summers with his mother's family in France. He was sent to Hill, a top prep (what the British would call 'public') school in Pennsylvania. It was while he was at Hill that he discovered his parents had split up. Lou Stone had maintained a constant stream of casual affairs, including prostitutes, while he buried himself in his work. Meanwhile his wife busied herself with entertaining on a grand scale, in both the expatriate French and New York arts circles; her own affairs followed. Young Oliver was even friendly with her lovers without realising their true status. Once split from his father, she got more fully into the scene, both in New York and in the South of France, and the teenaged Oliver was exposed to a lot of wild partying. Stone told biographer James Riordan that his mother was a good example of "the Sixties thing that happened among adults who, all of a sudden, felt so repressed by the Fifties that they wanted to explode." The shock of discovering the truth behind his parents' double lives was immense to Stone, as was his sense of alienation when forced to stay away in prep school. Emotionally, he felt abandoned.

Without delving too deeply into pop psychology, it is still easy to see the effect of both parents on Stone—and not just because he has addressed his father directly in *Wall Street*, his mother indirectly in *Heaven And Earth* and parodied the New York social scene bitterly in *The Doors*. Most of Stone's early films deal either with unformed characters forced to choose between parental figures or obsessive characters who initially reject the entire concept of parental (or marital) dependence.

Like his father, Stone wound up at Yale in 1965. He lost himself in literature, lasting one semester before having what he describes as a breakdown and taking a leave of absence. Influenced perhaps by reading *Lord Jim*, he joined an English teaching programme in Asia and was assigned to Saigon. It's odd how Joseph Conrad and Vietnam have knitted themselves together in the American psyche.

In Saigon, Stone found freedom from the all-male conformity of Hill and Yale. This was 1965 and American forces had reached the half-million mark. Stone was enthralled with the burgeoning prostitution scene in Saigon; he fell into a double life, teaching Chinese Catholic students by day and delving into Saigon's nightlife after dusk. But teaching bored him and he signed on an American merchant ship as a wiper. In 1966, he returned to the US on another merchantman and headed for Mexico where he spent four months working on a novel called *A Child's Night Dream*, a rambling rite of passage with Vietnam already becoming an obsession to him. He returned to New York and continued working on the book. Finally, at his father's urging, he returned to Yale but spent most of his time on the novel. He left without completing the semester and, when the novel failed to find a publisher in New York, threw half of it into the East River. In April 1967 he enlisted in the Army.

He had been known as William or Bill throughout his schooldays, but as a writer Stone preferred to be known as Oliver. Now, requesting assignment in the infantry, he once again became Bill Stone, about to put paid to the youngster who remained in some sense a true believer in his father's America. By September, he was on the ground in Vietnam.

Stone was a combat infantryman, unusual not only among the people who later wrote or made movies about Vietnam but also unusual among people from his privileged social status. He was wounded twice. He wrote constantly, discovered drugs and soul music. His father flew to Hong Kong and pulled strings to get him transferred to non-combat duty, but Stone refused and wound up with the Air Cavalry, where he joined a 'Lurp'—a long-range recon platoon—and met the sergeant who would be the model for Elias in *Platoon*. He received a Bronze Star for heroism in a moment whose sudden impulsiveness is reflected in a similar scene in *Platoon*. After leaving the Lurp unit he met his Sergeant Barnes character. In November 1968 his Vietnam tour ended. The preppie who believed in the establishment, in "truth, justice and the American way," had cut the ties to his upbringing and recreated his beliefs. "I realised that combat is totally random. Life is a matter of luck or destiny, take your pick…I became spiritual in Vietnam. Organised religion is for people who fear Hell but true spirituality is for people who've been to Hell. Possibly, I was saved for a reason…to write about the experience, maybe. To make a movie about it."

It would be some time before either the spirituality or the movie emerged. But William Stone had died in Vietnam and Oliver Stone was born there. Oliver was what his mother had always called him, so it was as if the Army had been his obligation to the values of his father's world and now he was free to choose his mother's.

Upon his discharge, he went to Mexico and was arrested re-entering the US still carrying some of his Vietnamese marijuana. He was jailed in San Diego, charged with smuggling. When he finally got to a phone, he called his father and Lou Stone's money eventually talked with the public defender, who quickly got the charges dismissed. The frustrations of his powerlessness and the flexibility of the system when plied with money would be reflected powerfully in *Midnight Express* and in the border scenes of *Salvador*.

Stone returned to New York where he continued to do drugs, became obsessed with Jim Morrison and with movies. He wrote a screenplay called *Break*, about his Vietnam experiences, and another called *Dominique* set in his mother's New York arty circle. Eventually he applied to NYU on the GI bill, taking a few classes until starting full time in the fall of 1969. He made three short student films: *Last Year In Vietnam* (a Vietnam veteran wanders the streets of New York and throws away his medals), *The Madman Of Martinique* (20 mins: Lou Stone gets killed in the subway) and *Michael And Marie*. They were very heavily influenced by the French New Wave, sharing their fascination with moving camera, hand-held shots and expressive black and white footage. His most influential teacher was Martin Scorsese.

As a student, Stone stood out from his fellows. Think of NYU as an urban *Animal House*; Stone was D-Day. It's not far-fetched to think that the image of him, dishevelled and obsessive in his army jacket, could have been a model for Travis Bickle in Scorsese's *Taxi Driver*. Once he'd finished at NYU, he supported himself by, among other things, driving a taxi.

He also met his first wife, Najwa Sarkis, a Lebanese-born woman who worked as a protocol attaché at the Moroccan embassy in New York. They were married in 1971, just before Stone finished at NYU. Sarkis would prove an incredibly supportive wife for Stone as he laboured over his screenplays. These included *Once Too Much*, about a student busted at the border carrying marijuana who's offered the choice between jail and Vietnam, and *The Wolves*, where a son returns in disguise to a Greek island to kill his stepfather before facing his brother who has arrived to find the killer. Stone was already recycling his life into film.

Finding actual work in film was more difficult. He had a small part in *Battle Of Love's Return* (1971) directed by his childhood friend Lloyd Kaufman. He also worked with Kaufman as an associate producer on a softcore porno film called *Sugar Cookies* (1973) directed by Theodore Gershuny with George Shannon, Mary Woronov and Monique Van Vooren. Along with two of his colleagues on the film, Stone formed a company called Euro-American Pictures and tried to get financing for another of his screenplays. It would be the beginning of a long apprenticeship in the business.

# 6: The Schlockmeister's Apprentice

Though his unproduced screenplays combined New Wave ideas with large themes and elements of classical tragedy, when Stone got the opportunity to actually direct he started with horror and, as he became expert at writing screenplays for hire, he concentrated on genre work. Exploitation cinema has, of course, always provided an entry ground for talented directors who delight in finding their ways around modest budgets and modest production values. Stone's experience in exploitation would also help him learn to shape his work for the bigger market-place. The film that began it all was called *Seizure*.

## Seizure (1974; aka Queen Of Evil)

*Cast:* Jonathan Frid (Edmund Blackstone), Christina Pickles (Nicole), Martine Beswick (Queen of Evil), Troy Donahue (Mark), Richard Cox (Gerald), Mary Woronov (Mikki), Joe Sirola (Charlie), Hervé Villechaize (Spider), Henry Baker (Jackal, the Giant Executioner), Roger de Koven (Serge); Anne Meacham, Timothy Ousey, Lucy Bingham.

*Crew:* Producers: Garrard Glenn, Jeffrey Kapelman (Cinerama/AIP); Screenplay: Edward Mann, Stone; Story: Stone; Photography: Roger Racine; Editors: Nobuko Oganesoff, Stone; Music: Lee Gagnon; Art Director: Najwa Stone; Edmund's sketches: Mann.

*Story:* Waiting for six friends to join them for the weekend, horror writer Edmund Blackstone tells his wife Nicole of his recurring nightmare. A radio broadcast warns that three members of a Manson-like family have escaped from an insane asylum. After his guests arrive Edmund finds his dog hanged. His son Jason sees a face at the window—one of the faces from Edmund's dreams. Edmund reveals the dream to Serge: the party will be invaded by a dwarf, a giant and the Queen of Evil. Vain Eunice kills herself after being disfigured by a face cream that Spider (the dwarf) promises will grant her eternal youth. Betsy, the maid, is killed by the Executioner. The Queen of Evil makes love to Mark, then kills him. When the rest discover the intruders an argument starts and Edmund accidentally shoots Gerald. The Queen announces that only one of those in the house will survive until dawn. Charlie loses a death race and is executed. His wife Mikki attempts to escape and is forced into a duel to the death with Edmund, which she loses. Serge suggests Edmund has, like Faust, called down the demons on them. Strengthened by his belief in God, Serge goes willingly to his execution. Edmund's wife, Nicole, blames Edmund then kills herself, asking only that he save their son. The Queen offers Edmund his life if he reveals where

Jason is hiding. Suspecting this is all a dream, he inadvertently gives it away. His wife's ghost saves the child. Edmund, being strangled, wakes up, saying, "I had the dream again, clearer than ever. But it's over." He is in bed with the Queen of Evil. Then Nicole sends Jason to wake his father before the guests arrive. Another radio report tells us Edmund has died of a heart attack, his body discovered by his son.

*Background:* Stone's screenplay, based on an actual dream, was written with Ed Mann and the money was raised from Canadian investors who, unfortunately, went bust before the film began shooting. Another producer stepped in, but in return for the finance took all the rights to the film which eventually had a limited release in the USA via Cinerama, the company that handled Hammer's horror movies. Hammer is a good comparison for the finished product in that a basically simple format attempts to transcend its budgetary constraints through imaginative film-making and good casting.

This pure 'B' movie horror film actually sets many of the creative templates of Stone's later work. He was able to assemble a cast of actors much better than the nature of the project or its $150,000 budget would lead you to expect and he gets some relatively strong performances from them. Frid was the star of the daytime vampire soap *Dark Shadows*, Donahue had been a teen matinee idol in the Fifties and Villechaize was a veteran of a Bond film and was an in-demand television actor. The male stars give the film its air of unreality but the women help anchor it, particularly Christina Pickles—always undervalued—as Edmund's wife and Mary Woronov, a veteran of Andy Warhol's factory. Martine Beswick as the Queen of Evil was another casting coup; she brings an unreal, more than human quality of evil beauty worthy of Barbara Steele at her very best but with a softer, more alluring edge.

She also helps delineate for Edmund a dilemma common to most Stone characters. The choice between Edmund's artistic drive, which is presented as a self-indulgent obsession, and his wife (and child) is symbolised by the choice between the blonde, pure wife and the dark-haired Queen of Evil. Stone's characters are almost always forced to choose between obsession and security, between the drive of their ego and their loved ones. If you'd like to read that dilemma into Stone's own life and his sense of its dark side…well, the tortured artist is named Black-Stone, isn't he?

*The Thumper:* It's all a dream, although there remains an element of ambiguity which will be more pronounced in Stone's next horror effort.

*The Verdict:* This is the kind of film which might have been a cult favourite with a little more budget and reasonable distribution. It has its strong points. 2/5

After finishing with *Seizure* Stone continued writing screenplays. Sergio Leone's westerns impressed him so much he wrote *The Ungodly*, intended as a vehicle for Charles Bronson, crossing Leone with an *El Topo* kind of mysticism. *Cover-Up* was based loosely on the Patty Hearst kidnapping. The kidnapping of a younger heiress is actually arranged by the FBI to discredit radical groups. The criminal hired to mastermind it balks at killing the girl and goes on the run with her. This script got passed to Robert Bolt, who persuaded producer Fernando Ghia to option it and invited Stone to Los Angeles. There Bolt helped him rewrite the script, but since Ghia could never sell the idea of such a film being directed by an unknown like Stone it never did get made. It was enough, however, to get him an agent at William Morris.

With Stone spending so much time in LA, the pressures on his marriage increased and he and his wife split in 1976; they would eventually divorce two years later. He returned to New York and collaborated on more screenplays, including one called *Rascals* about a struggling writer in New York. While he and his roommate were trying to get financing, Stone continued to turn out scripts. Ed Mann got him hired to adapt a Robin Moore novel, *Barkoon*, but that too went unproduced.

It was in 1976, perhaps inspired by the Bicentennial, that Stone wrote the first version of the script that would eventually become *Platoon*. He returned to LA where the script soon attracted the attention of producer Martin Bregman. Hollywood remained uninterested in downbeat Vietnam pictures, but the powerful story helped Stone's reputation grow and he was hired, at the insistence of Columbia's Peter Guber, to write the screenplay for Alan Parker's *Midnight Express*. Stone would bring many of the themes from *Platoon* to that story with great success.

## Midnight Express (director: Alan Parker, 1978)

*Cast:* Brad Davis (Billy Hayes), Randy Quaid (Jimmy Booth), John Hurt (Max), Irene Miracle (Susan), Bo Hopkins (Tex), Paul Smith (Hamidou), Norbert Weisser (Erich), Mike Kellin (Mr Hayes), Paolo Bonacelli (Rifki).

*Crew:* Producers: Alan Marshall, David Puttnam; Executive Producer: Peter Guber; Screenplay: Stone, based on the book by Billy Hayes with William Hoffer; Photography: Michael Seresin; Editor: Gerry Hambling; Music: Giorgio Moroder.

*Background:* Although the film generated controversy for its portrayal of the Turkish judicial and penal systems as violent and corrupt, at heart Stone's screenplay worked because it recognised that the basic conflict is Billy's own: his need to accept the wilder side of his nature and act in the world rather than simply rebel against his parents. That his escape is facilitated by the Turkish guard's attempt to convert him forcibly to the 'wild side' by homosexual rape heightens the drama of his being forced to make a choice and act.

This film can be seen as a dry run for many of the themes of *Platoon*. Erich, the Swede, is the prototype for Elias; think of Elias' enticing of Chris Taylor by blowing smoke down the gun barrel, not to mention his leering appraisals, in the context of the Swede's homosexual proposition. Billy's escape comes after he first goes wild, gouging Rifki's eye (the eyeball will reappear, even more gratuitously, in *Any Given Sunday*) and biting off his tongue, and then kills Hamidou, the most violent of the characters. It is an almost exact foreshadowing of Chris' explosion in the climactic firefight and his killing of Barnes. Indeed, Billy's outbursts in the Turkish court have the same function as the summing-up in *Platoon*: to root the story in one innocent smuggler's experience reminiscent of Stone's own arrest at the Mexican border. Its aim is not to present a polemic about the Turkish justice system.

Other scenes have particular resonance: Billy's reaction to Susan's desperate query—"What can I do for you?"—is to have her display her breasts while he masturbates. It not only reveals Billy's condition brilliantly, it is pure Stone in its exploitative excess. The scenes with Mike Kellin as Billy's father also have a very real sense of helplessness which questions an entire value system and echoes Stone's own experience in a San Diego jail. Kellin can be compared to Martin Sheen's parental rôle in *Wall Street* or, the reversal of the scene, when the father visits his daughters in *Heaven And Earth*.

*The Verdict:* Parker, if anything, softens Stone's approach, but the film remains powerful. 3/5

*Midnight Express* would win Stone an Oscar for Best Adapted Screenplay. While it was being shot, Bregman brought him back to New York to work on the adaptation of a Vietnam movie based on disabled veteran Ron Kovic's memoir, *Born On The Fourth Of July*. The original plan was for Al Pacino to star and William Friedkin to direct. Ironically, the film didn't get made at the time because of the two films which dominated the Oscars the year Stone won, *The Deer Hunter* and *Coming Home*. Both dealt with Vietnam from the perspective of the home front, *Coming Home*, starring Jon Voight as a sensitive paraplegic, covered the very same ground as Kovic's book (in fact, Kovic served as an advisor on it). Unlike *The Deer Hunter*, *Coming Home* was not a box-office hit. By then director Dan Petrie had replaced Friedkin and had gone as far as shooting tests with Pacino in a wheelchair, but Pacino, worried that a similar story would bomb even worse, left the project. Kovic was shattered by the experience, but he and Stone would remain close, and the film would finally get made with Stone helming it.

The immediate effect of his Oscar was more pronounced on Stone himself than it was on his career. His already intense Hollywood party life got an exponential boost. His wildman persona, which involved large quantities of drugs and a willingness to push the limits of any situation, wasn't always the best formula for making friends and generating more work. In the words of his agent Ron Mardigan, "he didn't care if you thought he was an asshole, as long as you thought he was a talented asshole." He actually returned a $250,000 fee rather than write an adaptation of a P D James mystery because he hated the material so much.

Around this time, he was hired by producer Edward Pressman to adapt *Conan the Barbarian*, yet another screenplay which would not get produced quickly. He also met Richard Rutkowski, while doing research on an adaptation of a prison novel called *Baby Boy*. Rutkowski had known Jim Morrison and the two discovered a shared interest in mind-expanding spiritual quests. Rutkowski would become a frequent Stone collaborator, as producer, co-writer, actor and running mate on his spiritual indulgences.

Meanwhile, the release of *Apocalypse Now,* for all its success, was making Hollywood even more wary of Vietnam war epics. Stone had an Oscar but he was going nowhere in Hollywood so he travelled to Europe, losing himself in Poland and Holland.

In 1979, back in Hollywood, he met Elizabeth Cox, a Texas-born all-American girl. They quickly moved in together. She began typing his scripts and, like his first wife, "taking care of him." In light of the role of women in Stone's films, it is interesting that she is often billed on Stone's films, first as the 'director's assistant' and later—from *Wall Street* on—as "Naijo No Ko" which is Japanese for "success from inside help." Makes a change from 'trouble and strife'.

Stone had received an offer from Orion to write and direct a picture within a limited budget. He brought in Pressman to produce, intending to make *Baby Boy,* but soon decided that the prison story was too unrealistic. Instead he directed an adaptation of a novel about an artist tormented by his severed hand.

## The Hand (1981)

*Cast:* Michael Caine (Jon Lansdale), Andrea Marcovicci (Anne Lansdale), Annie McEnroe (Stella Roche), Bruce McGill (Brian Ferguson), Viveca Lindfors (Doctress), Rosemary Murphy (Karen Wagner), Mara

Hobel (Lizzie), Pat Corley (Sheriff), Nicholas Hormann (Bill Richman), Stone (Bum).

*Crew:* Producer: Edward Pressman (Orion/Warner Bros./Pressman-Ixtlan); Executive Producer: Clark Paylow; Screenplay: Stone, based on the book *The Lizard's Tail* by Marc Brandel; Photography: King Baggot; Editor: Richard Marks; Music: James Horner; Production Design: John Michael Riva; Special Effects: Carlo Rambaldi.

*Story:* Jon Lansdale draws Mandro, a superhero comic. His wife Anne is bored with life in the country. While chopping wood with his daughter, he cuts off a lizard's tail; the lizard keeps moving which, he explains, is "only a reflex." As he and his wife argue on the way to a dinner party, a freak accident shears off his right hand.

No one can find the severed hand; according to his daughter "Mommy says it ran away." Unable to work with only his left hand, Lansdale returns to the accident scene where he finds his signet ring…and is watched by his other hand.

Moving to the city, his agent arranges for him to continue to write continuity for the strip while a new artist draws it and presents him with an offer to teach. Unhappy, he watches as his wife and her New Age instructor grow closer. They argue. The hand returns, retrieving its ring. Lansdale is fitted with a prosthetic hand but will never draw again. He doesn't like the new artist's work which they discover has been mutilated (by the hand). Leaving the office, he pushes away a similarly handless bum. The hand chokes the bum to death in an alley. He returns home to find his wife on her knees, crying, with her instructor, but she won't discuss why. He takes the teaching job in California and Anne insists on a trial separation, waiting until Christmas to join him. The hand follows Lansdale who finds his missing ring on his pillow.

He begins an affair with Stella, one of his students, while confessing to McGill, a psychology professor, that he may be suffering blackouts. He has found a drawing of a hand and a naked woman he can't remember doing. He becomes jealous of Stella and McGill. The hand strangles her. His wife and daughter arrive and it's obvious her relationship with the instructor has deepened. He discovers his jealousy of McGill was mistaken. The hand chokes McGill. His wife announces that she is returning to New York and taking their daughter. The hand strangles her and, as Lansdale tells his daughter to call the police, the hand attacks him. He wounds it.

He is revived by medics. His wife and daughter are OK, but the police discover the bodies of Stella and McGill in his car boot. Lansdale receives therapy, strapped to an EEG machine. The hand attacks the therapist. He pulls off the restraints, laughing.

*Background:* As Stone himself has noted, it was typical of Hollywood that, after his success with *Midnight Express*, the first film he managed to direct turned out to be a horror film very much like *Seizure*. Both films concern artists who may be engendering the entire world of horror that menaces them because of their own mental instability. Where in *Seizure* everything may be Blackstone's dream, here Lansdale's blackouts provide a similar element of ambiguity, which in itself should have been enough to produce psychological horror. But the finished product is torn between that sort of psychology—the mental horror of Lansdale's jealous breakdown—and the actual horror of the hand, for which there was a long tradition that perhaps did not need revisiting.

Not surprisingly, the studio (who had the final cut) were more inclined towards the latter strand. This conflict is reflected in the basic pull of the picture: Lansdale is another of Stone's obsessive artists torn between the demands of his creativity and his family. As with many Stone heroes, he actively seeks out a female alternative to the demanding wife who both drains his creative energies and seeks to develop on her own with her New Age classes. Stella, on the other hand, drives Lansdale to new creative impulses (as well as destructive ones).

The film looks good and James Horner's score is excellent. Michael Caine and Stone apparently got on well, although Caine was constantly having to reassure the neophyte director. Stone was into his heaviest drug phase at the time, freebasing cocaine, but throughout his career, his incredible stamina has meant that his manic partying has not affected production schedules adversely.

*Reptiles Under Stones:* Given his fascination with snakes and lizards, I wonder if Stone's original interest was sparked simply by the title of Brandel's novel, *The Lizard's Tail*?

*Barbarian Artists:* The Mandro art was actually produced by Barry Windsor-Smith, who had made his name drawing Marvel's *Conan the Barbarian* comic book. He would turn up again, doing storyboards for the first Conan film when it was finally produced.

*The Thumper:* Although the lizard scene gives it all away and Viveca Lindfors provides a comic summing-up, this may be Stone's least didactic ending. You can believe the hand is real, or not.

*The Verdict:* What is the sound of one Hand clapping? 2/5

Ed Pressman had acquired the film rights to the Conan character based on the pulp magazine stories of Robert E Howard. He thought Stone would be the perfect choice to write and direct the sword-and-sorcery story of the barbarian from Cimmeria in Howard's Hyborean Age.

# Conan The Barbarian (director: John Milius, 1982)

*Cast:* Arnold Schwarzenegger (Conan), James Earl Jones (Thulsa Doom), Sandahl Bergman (Valeria), Gerry Lopez (Subotai), Max Von Sydow (King Osric), Ben Davidson (Rexor), Cassandra Gaviola (The Witch).

*Crew:* Executive Producer: Dino De Laurentiis; Producer: Edward R Pressman; Screenplay: Stone & John Milius, based on Robert E Howard; Photography: Duke Callaghan; Editor: Timothy O'Meara; Music: Basil Poledouris; Production Design: Ron Cobb.

*Background:* Stone's *Platoon* was still a formidable spec script and he had his Oscar win behind him. Paperback reprints of the Conan stories had taken off in the Sixties fantasy boom which the paperback editions of *The Lord Of The Rings* inspired (what comes around, etc.) and a popular Marvel comic book, originally with Roy Thomas adapting the stories for Barry Windsor-Smith to draw, had given the character even more exposure. Pressman considered giving Stone the chance to co-direct with Joe Alves, who had been second unit director on *Jaws*. But producer Dino De Laurentiis bought the idea, with Stone's script, and wanted an experienced hand for what promised to be a big-budget production. The first director he approached was Ridley Scott who worked briefly on the script with Stone. But when Scott pulled out to make *Blade Runner*, the film was handed to John Milius whose credits included the screenplay of *Apocalypse Now* and directing the surfing epic *Big Wednesday* and, closer to home, *The Wind And The Lion*. According to Stone, Milius tore up all his notes, rewrote the script, and that was that.

Actually, Milius' version sticks fairly close to Stone's original first half of the film while expanding Conan's origin story. But Stone's version, inspired by Howard's tales tracing Conan's progress from Barbarian to King, would have ended with Conan's forces battling Thulsa Doom's legions from Hell in a massive Armageddon, a sort of Hyborean Age *Apocalypse Then*. Milius, concentrating on the snake cult (another of Stone's reptilian images?), kept the focus more on Conan the individual and thus brought Arnold Schwarzenegger to stardom.

*The Verdict:* It still holds up pretty well, though Scott's version might've been more fun to look at, and Stone's apocalyptic Hyborean battle might have been more challenging to make. 3/5

# Scarface (director: Brian De Palma, 1983)

*Cast:* Al Pacino (Tony Montana), Michelle Pfeiffer (Elvira), Mary Elizabeth Mastrantonio (Gina Montana), Robert Loggia (Frank Lopez), F Murray Abraham (Omar Suarez), Steven Bauer (Manuel Ray), Miriam Colon (Mama), Paul Shenar (Alejando Sosa), Harris Yulin (Bernstein), Ángel Salazar (Chi Chi), Pepe Serna (Angel Fernandez).

*Crew:* Producer: Martin Bregman; Screenplay: Stone; Photography: John Alonzo; Editors: Jerry Greenberg, David Ray; Music: Giorgio Moroder.

*Background:* Stone had a serious drug problem when he was asked to do *Scarface* and perhaps the opportunity to research the drug trade first-hand appealed to him. He had also been involved in writing a screenplay called *Inside The Cocaine Wars.* His research helped convince him to quit drugs altogether, so he and Elizabeth, whom he had married after finishing *The Hand,* moved to Paris where they quit cocaine cold turkey. Stone wrote with heavy drapes blocking the sunlight from their apartment's skylight. He called the script "getting even with cocaine."

Seen as a farewell to the excesses of the drug era, *Scarface* is an impressive script. The finished product is probably the closest of any of the films based on his screenplays to one of his own films, in part because of De Palma's own preference for cinematic flash and excitement which, if anything, highlights the elements of over-the-top black comedy. Tony Montana is already a typical Stone wild man when he arrives in the USA; it takes a mountain of coke and a pile of bodies to then turn Al Pacino into James Woods. He faces the kind of parental dilemma most Stone heroes face—in his case he has to kill his father figure and marry, as it were, his mother (the father figure's woman). The Shakespearean element in this may seem heavy-handed but Stone insists it was *Richard III*, with the attractive yet appalling villain, that was his model, not *Hamlet.* And remember, Richard marries the widow of a man he has killed.

This is all confused, of course, by his incestuous longing for his sister, a sub-plot which was handled with far more frankness and sizzle in the original *Scarface* (1932). But here the choice between purity and family is presented by the sizzling dark-haired woman while the descent into madness is linked to the icy blonde.

Sidney Lumet had originally been scheduled to direct the film as a period remake but Lumet wanted to update it, to draw the parallel between the prohibition era with alcohol and the current prohibition era of drugs. Like Pacino, he already knew Stone, but after seeing Stone's script he backed out, largely because of the violence. The connection resonates because

Lumet won an Oscar for directing Paddy Chayevsky's script of *Network,* and *Scarface* is far closer to the tone of that film than virtually any of Stone's films until *Natural Born Killers.*

Both Bregman and Pacino liked the script. Lumet was replaced by Brian De Palma who, as discussed before, simply took what was on the page at surface value and ran with it. Looking back, we might argue that *Natural Born Killers* is Stone's most Brian De Palma-like film.

Even with cuts, the film runs three hours and ran well over budget; Stone's fee was $300,000. It wasn't a smash hit, which Stone attributes to having a bad guy as the hero, but it has reached cult status and certainly was the inspiration for the hit TV series *Miami Vice* as well as any number of gangster pictures which followed.

*The Thumper:* "You fuckin fuck with me and I'll fuckin fuck you up, you fuck."

*The Verdict:* Stone said "the paranoia of coke is the most striking aspect—the fire of it," and I've always liked to see *Scarface* as an allegory of Hollywood in the Eighties, with Tony Montana being a stand-in for any number of coke-fuelled film-makers whose movies and dreams got more grandiose in direct proportion to the amount of powder that lands on their glass table tops. If, as Stone has also said, "luxury is corruption," whatever applies to Miami applies in spades to Hollywood. 4/5

Stone continued churning out screenplays and searching for his chance to direct. It was the promise of just such a chance that led him to working on his next big project and, again, he would be disappointed by Dino De Laurentiis.

## Year Of The Dragon (director: Michael Cimino, 1985)

*Cast:* Mickey Rourke (Stanley White), John Lone (Joey Tai), Ariane (Tracey Tzu), Caroline Kava (Connie White), Leonard Termo (Angelo Rizzo), Ray Barry (Louis Bukowski), Eddie Jones (William McKenna), Joey Chin (Ronnie Chang), Victor Wong (Harry Yung), Fan Mui Sang (White Powder Ma).

*Crew:* Producer: Dino De Laurentiis; Screenplay: Stone & Cimino, based on the book by Robert Daley; Photography: Alex Thomson; Editor: Françoise Bonnot; Production Design: Wolf Kroeger; Music: David Mansfield.

*Background:* Michael Cimino had been a long-time champion of Stone's script of *Platoon* and proposed to Stone that he co-write *Year Of The Dragon* for only $200,000—well below the going rate for an Oscar-winning screenwriter with his successes—in return for producer Dino De Laurentiis' promise that he would finance *Platoon* with Stone directing. That De Laurentiis had handed his *Conan* screenplay to Milius didn't seem to bother Stone, who was already becoming inured to the ways of Hollywood business. On the other hand, Cimino might also have felt that the presence of Stone, still hot from *Scarface*, might help facilitate his comeback from the financial disaster that was *Heaven's Gate*.

Stanley White, of course, is a Vietnam veteran and Vietnam informs much of the film as White's obsession is re-fighting and winning that conflict in New York. In the novel, his concerns were more personal, trying to save his career. Stone has made him a more obsessive character who forms a link between Tony Montana, who is all id, and Richard Boyle, who can be saved by Maria's love. In the films that followed, *Salvador*, Stone would be careful, perhaps too much so, to root his characters' motivations in the personal.

Eventually, White has to choose, in effect, between his wife (who gets murdered) and his affair with an Asian TV reporter (who gets gang-raped), a very Stonian way of symbolising his choice between rage at the Vietnamese or acceptance of American society which has incorporated Asians. It is also the first, and most vicious, manifestation of his on-going love/hate relationship with television news. The accusations of racism against the film seem to be founded solely on taking in the surface of Mickey Rourke's performance rather than putting the character into context. Interestingly, in the original screenplay, White traps the villain (John Lone) into being arrested for bigamy after he brings his Chinese wife to America. In Dino's version, they shoot it out on a railroad bridge by the docks.

Lone, who is almost an anti-hero in this film, is yet another Stone figure brought down by making the wrong choice. In the finished film, Lone's status as yang to Mickey Rourke's yin is emphasised by that stylised final shoot-out. It, and the opening shoot-out in the Chinese restaurant, may have been a reverse influence on a number of Hong Kong thrillers in their late Eighties worldwide boom.

*The Verdict:* Rourke is way too young for the rôle but he still carries it off with an energy which makes you want to believe in it. You also want to believe that such a jerk could somehow appeal to Ariane, but you never really do. She is, however, the most convincing of the many news reporters in Stone's films (but still not *that* convincing). 3/5

After *Year Of The Dragon,* Stone worked on another adaptation of a New York crime novel, this time for director Hal Ashby. *Eight Million Ways To*

*Die* would give him a salutary lesson in the pitfalls of Hollywood excess on a good story.

## Eight Million Ways To Die (director: Hal Ashby, 1985)

*Cast:* Jeff Bridges (Matt Scudder), Rosanna Arquette (Sarah), Alexandra Paul (Sunny), Andy Garcia (Angel), Randy Brooks (Chance).

*Crew:* Producer: Steve Roth; Screenplay: Stone & David Lee Henry, based on the novel by Lawrence Block; Photography: Stephen H Burum; Music: James Newton Howard.

*Background:* Lawrence Block's Matt Scudder novels are set in New York's Hell's Kitchen and Scudder's burnt-out ex-cop has a very specific New York sense of moral relativism. Apart from a strong sense of restraint, he is in every other way a perfect Oliver Stone hero. Stone's original script, however, was heavily rewritten (primarily by Robert Towne) and the setting shifted to LA. Although the finished product remains watchable, it lacks most of Scudder's original edge and, apart from a few touches of excess (particularly in the hooker's scenes and in the hostage scenes), very little of Stone's trademark dynamism. There is the choice of women, between Scudder's demanding wife (who wants him to stop drinking) and the whore with the heart of gold. Interestingly, it is Scudder's desire to fulfil his responsibility as a father (he stops to buy a gift for his daughter) which leads to the death of another whore, Sunny, the device that moves the entire plot.

*The Verdict:* Interesting and watchable to a point, but a big waste of the character of Scudder. 2/5

The Dino De Laurentiis deal to write and direct *Platoon* in return for the bargain screenplay for *Year Of The Dragon* fell through when De Laurentiis couldn't find a distributor who would make the relatively small investment necessary to handle the film. Stone had already spent considerable development money on casting and doing location scouting in the Philippines and De Laurentiis now said that unless the money were repaid, all rights to the script would remain his. Stone had not only lost his chance to direct, he appeared to have lost his most personal script as well.

His son Sean was born in December 1984; around the same time, visiting his friend Richard Boyle, he found Boyle's notes for a book about his adventures as a foreign correspondent in El Salvador. He began working with Boyle on the script and travelled to El Salvador to research and scout locations. In March 1985, Lou Stone died in New York. As if energised in a business sense by the death of his father, Stone and his lawyers got back the rights to *Platoon* by threatening suits that could have held up the release of

*Dragon.* It was then that producer Gerald Green passed Stone's script for *Salvador* to John Daly, the colourful former pop and boxing promoter whose Hemdale Films was prepared to finance both it and *Platoon.* Oliver Stone's directing career was about to be launched.

*Note:* The analysis which follows is not strictly chronological. The twelve films have been grouped into four trilogies, suggested by their subject matter. A closer look, however, reveals that the trilogies fall almost into chronological sequence, apart from the Vietnam films, which are spaced out among the others, and *Natural Born Killers,* which jumps the gun on the Nineties before *Nixon* ends the Sixties. This reflects the lingering power of Vietnam within Stone and the way it has taken him much time and thought to finally come to grips with the expression of his experiences.

# 7: The Eighties Trilogy

What unites these three films is the way they capture the essence of the American political landscape under the Reagan regime. *Salvador*, for all its balance, pulls no punches regarding the involvement of the US government in both crime and cover-up; *Wall Street* reacts to the "big swinging dicks" of junkbond USA before Tom Wolfe even noticed their contrasting collars; and *Talk Radio* not only jumps on a media phenomenon of the Eighties the same way *Natural Born Killers* does for the Nineties but also reflects John Mitchell's famous, and chillingly accurate prediction after Watergate that "this country is going so far to the right you won't even recognise it."

To keep chronological perspective, note that *Salvador* and *Platoon* were both released (in that order) in 1986; Stone competed against himself for the best screenplay Oscar which he won for *Platoon*. *Salvador* remains the more impressive film and while James Woods' loss of the best-actor Oscar to Paul Newman in *The Colour Of Money* is understandable in terms of Oscar sentiments, it seems very sad indeed.

## Salvador (1986)

*Cast:* James Woods (Richard Boyle), James Belushi (Dr Rock), Michael Murphy (Ambassador Kelly), John Savage (Cassady), Elpidia Carrillo (Maria), Tony Plana (Major Max), Colby Chester (Jack Morgan), Cindy Gibb (Cathy Moore), Will MacMillan (Colonel Hyde), Valerie Wildman (Pauline Axelrod), Jose Carlos Ruiz (Archbishop Romero), Jorge Luke (Colonel Figueroa), Miguel Ehrenberg (Captain Marti), Juan Fernandez (Lieutenant), Garry Farr (Australian Reporter), Rosario Zuniga (Max's Assistant), Maria Rubell (Boyle's wife), Sean Stone (Boyle's baby).

*Crew:* Executive Producers: John Daly, Derek Gibson; Producers: Gerald Green, Stone (Hemdale); Screenplay: Stone, Richard Boyle; Photography: Robert Richardson, Leon Sanchez Ruiz (Mexico); Editor: Claire Simpson; Music: Georges Delerue; Production Design: Bruno Rubeo.

*Story:* Photojournalist Richard Boyle hears reports on killings in El Salvador but needs money to return there as well as pay his overdue rent. When he is arrested for various motor-vehicle violations, his DJ friend Dr Rock bails him out. Discovering his Italian wife has left him and taken their son back to Italy, Boyle convinces Rock, whose wife has kicked him out and whose dog has been killed at the pound, to head to Salvador. They are stopped at the border and threatened by soldiers, but Boyle's flattering profile of Colonel Figueroa, written during the Salvador/Guatemala 'soccer war' becomes their passport to San Salvador. Boyle is reunited with his mistress, Maria, and her two children and with photojournalist John Cassady. While Boyle tries to contact the left-wing guerrillas, right-wing Major Max prepares to assassinate Archbishop Romero who is publicly anti-government. After Maria's brother Carlos and his friends mock Major Max on TV, Carlos and Rock are arrested; Boyle manages to bribe Rock free but Carlos disappears. With the help of Cathy Moore, an American Catholic lay worker, he tries to get Ambassador Kelly to help him find Carlos and arrange a *cedula*—a stamp showing you've voted in the virtually all right-wing elections; failure to have one is punishable by death squads—for Maria. Boyle, although still married, offers to marry Maria and at her insistence goes to confession at the cathedral, after which Romero is assassinated. Cassady photographs Romero's murder but his cameras are seized and Alvarez, a human-rights activist, is arrested for the killing. Carlos' body turns up, mutilated by torture, and Boyle is saved from a death squad by Cassady's intervention. Moore, picking up three nuns at the airport, is raped and killed by a death squad. US military adviser Colonel Hyde tries to cover up the murders, helped unwittingly by the 'balanced' reporting of network TV reporter Pauline Axelrod, but Kelly, who knows Moore, orders military aid to the regime to be cut off.

Boyle and Cassady meet the guerrillas in the mountains, and prepare a story on them. Still trying to barter for papers for Maria, Boyle shows Hyde and analyst Jack Morgan his pictures, proving they are not being armed by foreign elements. The guerrillas take Santa Ana; Boyle and Cassady photograph the battle. Hyde and Morgan lie to Kelly about the rebels and get him to restore aid and Figueroa drives off the guerrillas. Cassady is killed getting a shot of a strafing aeroplane. Boyle is wounded trying to save him and Cassady gives him pictures of rebels executing government soldiers. Rock obtains forged papers for Boyle and Maria. At the border, Boyle is about to be killed under orders from Major Max, but Rock manages to track down Kelly, who has been replaced by the new Reagan administration. Kelly's intervention saves Boyle. He sneaks Maria and the children into the US through the Mexican border, but their bus is stopped by US immigration and Maria and the children deported. End titles tell us that Maria survived and Boyle is still looking for her in refugee camps; that Cassady's photos were published; and that El Salvador remains one of the US' largest recipients of military aid.

*Background:* When Stone and Boyle originally headed for El Salvador, Stone was struck by its similarities to Vietnam in the build-up years of American involvement. They originally had the support of the Salvadorian government based on a version of the script which ended with the army destroying the rebels in the climactic battle. But the military adviser on the film, Colonel Ricardo Cienfuegos, was assassinated while playing tennis (note the tennis shots in the film) and President Duarte withdrew support.

*Salvador* followed in the wake of *Under Fire*, Roger Spottiswoode's account (written by Ron Shelton) of a photojournalist forced to eventually take sides in the Nicaragua war. That film had not been a hit and another film critical of US policy in Latin America was unlikely to make an impact at the box office. Stone had been considering the project on a low budget and even with Boyle playing himself. But Daly, who had co-promoted the Ali-Foreman fight in Zaire and whose Hemdale Films (in partnership with David Hemmings) had had a massive success with *Terminator*, was impressed with the force of the screenplays for *Salvador* and *Platoon* and willing to bankroll both with Stone directing. Perhaps *Salvador* seemed more bankable to a British company because US policy in Central America was probably receiving more attention in Britain than in the USA. *Salvador* was budgeted at $3.5 million with filming shifted to Mexico. This was enough for a quality cast and enough extras to shoot battle scenes, although Stone actually spent $4.5 million.

That the film looks far better than its budget may be the result of Stone beginning his long association with Robert Richardson, who was hired primarily on the strength of a BBC TV documentary, *Crossfire*—shot in El Salvador—and some re-shoots for Alex Cox's *Repo Man*. Stone had originally intended to cast Martin Sheen as Boyle and James Woods as Doc Rock, but Woods fell in love with the part of Boyle and the switch was crucial: Woods' energy propels the film, and his ambiguity and willingness to be unloved make it work.

There are some superb set piece scenes where Stone's film school background comes to the fore and Richardson delivers the goods. The cavalry charge of the rebels and the retaking of Santa Ana (with its overtones of the Alamo from US history) is followed by a wonderful shot of fleeing campesinos running past an old man carrying a dead or badly wounded child. Then we see a crying child still clutching a dead arm. The echoes of the shots start with Eisenstein, but in fairness that's not the first thought when one sees them and only comes on reflection.

*Salvador* is the film where Stone is most free with the use of humour to undercut the drama and violence of the story. It helps that he has Woods' fast-talking weasel and Belushi's drug-addled rocker (perhaps inspired by Hunter Thompson and sidekick in *Fear And Loathing*?). Belushi gets the great lines: "Who could leave all this?" as they survey the dingy flat Boyle's wife has abandoned, or "Screwing dogs, pigs in the street…it's like Baltimore." But moments like Woods negotiating his penance with the priest who takes his confession add humanity to his character and relief from the anguish outside. Boyle is another of many Stone heroes who survives on chutzpah but wonders if it is all worthwhile (Tony Montana's speculations on "is this what I kill for?" were a prototype).

*Choosing Salvation:* Salvador, of course, means 'saviour' and although the film is a moving portrayal of injustice and revolution, the real story is Boyle's salvation. His redemption, which comes through the love of Maria, the sacrificial death of Moore and the death of Cassady, occurs with the same sort of beatific grace as Elias' in platoon. The transformation of Boyle from sleazebag to human is still Stone's most poignant.

*Madonnas and Whores and Cops:* Stone's relation to women, already under some fire from his screenplays, remains problematic here. Our early encounters with women show them as either screaming harridans (Boyle's wife, who seems far more volatile than he is) or figures of authority (note that the traffic cop, the jailer and the 'executioner' at the dog pound are all women). We also see that when the rebels are executing government troops, the executions are carried out by a woman.

On arrival in Salvador, all the young women are either whores (which is, according to Boyle, the best reason to be there) or Madonnas, like aid worker Moore or Carmen. TV reporter Axelrod is accused of sleeping her way to the top at her network. The ultimate Madonna, of course, is Maria, an innocent who exists primarily to be loved; as his salvation, she insists on proper Catholicism from Boyle even though, on the surface, she is part of his corruption. Elpidia Carrillo manages to invest the rôle, which as written resembles Brando's Tahitian babe in *Mutiny On The Bounty*, with more depth. Although marrying Maria would make him a bigamist, Boyle also 'marries' Moore by giving her his ring as she lies dead.

It was Cindy Gibb's portrayal of Moore that Stone most often cites as a positive example of his roles for women, and she is very good. But, significantly, she is raped and killed and we last see her accepting the inevitable from the point of view of the rapist as she crosses herself and prays. It is both moving and exploitative.

*Choice Cuts:* The most infamous of the scenes deleted from the final cut was an orgy scene with an Army colonel. While Dr Rock gets a blow job from a hooker under the table, the colonel is screwing another hooker while he throws severed human ears into a champagne glass, saying "left-wing ears, right-wing ears, who gives a fuck." The scene recalls Carolyn Forché's poem 'The Colonel', collected in her prize-winning 1981 book *The Country Between Us*, itself based on a true incident which entered Central American reporting myth.

*It's Only TV:* Stone has a continuing love/hate relationship with network TV and its reporters (he would play one in *Born On The Fourth Of July*) and

Pauline Axelrod (a name suggestive of more sexuality than the reporter projects) is almost a prototype for Wayne Gale. She is presented in sharp contrast to Boyle, fastidiously neat and always framing her story within the balanced lines of received wisdom from the US, never questioning the basic assumptions of such questions. And, as is usually the case with Hollywood's TV reporters, she does her interviews and stand-ups with the arriving US 'trainers' in a manner that no reporter would ever get usable footage from (remember Michelle Pfeiffer in the otherwise forgettable *Up Close And Personal* broadcasting live from a prison riot much like *Natural Born Killers*', using an ENG camera with no cable or RF transmitter to get its signal beyond its own recorder?).

This contempt for the shallowness of network news and the pseudo-show-business mindset of its presenters would be a factor in some of the film's negative response and would be something that continued through *JFK* and *Natural Born Killers*. Stone reiterates the point by having Boyle refer constantly to Sidney Schanberg, the *New York Times* reporter who won a Pulitzer prize for his reporting from Cambodia (as portrayed in *The Killing Fields*). Schanberg reported from his hotel roof while Boyle was on the ground and the last American out.

On the other hand, Stone's portrayal of Boyle rings accurate for anyone who's worked in foreign reporting where quick thinking and fast talking on the ground are often the most important skills. So too does the characterisation of Cassady, who's in love with the danger of his job as we see from his expressions during the battle.

*The Thumper:* Boyle's speech to spooks Hyde and Morgan where he sets out his political agenda, including his belief in the American way, starts flags waving and fireworks bursting in the air. It grinds the film to a halt and swings Boyle for a moment from cynic to idealist (cynics are idealists who can't accept their ideals are often unreachable) to the point where he becomes holier than thou—not just to the two spooks but to the audience too. In the rest of the film, Boyle's moments of redemption are purely on the personal not the political level. Stone manages to undercut this, however, by having Hyde give Boyle the low-down immediately afterward which brings all of us back to reality.

A similar process takes place in one of the film's best scenes: after Boyle's last-second reprieve from execution, which borders on the melodramatic, Stone then sets Boyle to drinking happily with his almost-killers, even showing them (in a perfectly Boylean moment) the films hidden in his boot. This reinforcement of Boyle's essential anchoring in the moment makes the preceding scene ring true.

*The Verdict: Salvador* remains Stone's most emotionally-rich work, with politics and personal finely balanced. The large scale and small scale fit together and in James Woods' Boyle Stone created one of the great anti-heroes of Eighties cinema. 5/5

## Wall Street (1987)

*Cast:* Michael Douglas (Gordon Gekko), Charlie Sheen (Bud Fox), Darryl Hannah (Darien Taylor), Martin Sheen (Carl Fox), Terence Stamp (Sir Larry Wildman), Hal Holbrook (Lou Mannheim), Sean Young (Kate Gekko), Richard Dysart (Cromwell), Saul Rubinek (Harold Salt), Sylvia Miles (Realtor), Annie McEnroe (Muffie), James Spader (Roger Barnes), John C McGinley (Marvin), Chuck Pfeiffer (Chuckie), Tamara Tunie (Caroline), Franklin Cover (Dan), Josh Mostel (Ollie), Cecelia Peck (Candice Rogers), Paul Gulifoyle (Stone Livingston), Millie Perkins (Mrs Fox), Monique Van Vooren (Woman at 21), Andrea Thompson (Hooker), Michael O'Donoghue (Reporter), Jeff Beck (Investment Banker), Marlena Bileinska (Girl on Plane), Astrid de Richmonte (Au Pair).

*Crew:* Producer: Edward R Pressman (20th Century Fox/Pressman); Co-produder: A Kitman Ho; Screenplay: Stanley Weiser, Stone; Dialogue consultant: Liz Dixon; Photography: Robert Richardson; Second Unit: Tom Sigel; Editor: Claire Simpson; Associate Editors: David Brenner (LA), Joe Hutshing (NY); Production Design: Stephen Hendrickson; Music: Stewart Copeland.

*Story:* Broker Bud Fox, desperate to land corporate raider Gordon Gekko as a client, tips him about an FAA ruling affecting the airline where his father is a union representative. When the tip pays off, Gekko gives Bud a million dollars to invest for him. When Bud loses the money, Gekko coerces him into getting confidential information about his rival, Sir Larry Wildman; Bud disguises himself as a janitor to pilfer files that enable Gekko to block Wildman's takeover of a steel company. An incensed Wildman confronts Gekko at home and buys the shares from him—to Gekko's profit. Gekko uses Bud to buy stock for a hostile takeover but protects himself from anything Bud does by having him sign power-of-attorney forms. Bud gets Roger Barnes, a college friend, to hide his dealings, which are paid into offshore accounts. Bud buys a million-dollar apartment and Gekko's ex-girlfriend, Darien, decorates it; they begin an affair. Gekko decides to take over the airline where Bud's father works; only Carl Fox opposes the plan. Bud sides with Gekko until he realises—after he learns that the airline is being liquidated and the union pension fund cashed in—that Gekko has used him. His father has a heart attack. Bud approaches Wildman with an offer for revenge against Gekko provided he guarantees to keep the airline running. The plan works, but Bud and Barnes are arrested by the Security and Exchange commission. Bud wears a wire when he meets Gekko in Central Park. Gekko, losing his temper and attacking Bud, incriminates himself in the illegal transactions. Headed to the courthouse with his parents, who congratulate him on doing the right thing, Bud accepts that he will have to serve time in jail.

*Background:* "Greed is good" became as much a mantra for the 1980s as Clint Eastwood's "Make my day," but *Wall Street* is far from a simple satire of that era. In fact, in its essential ambiguity, its pulling of punches and its ultimate reliance on a narrow personal  (as opposed to a public polemical) agenda, it is possibly the most revealing of Stone's films.

Examine Gekko's "greed is good" speech closely and you'll find he makes better arguments against the capitalist system than for it. He says "greed is good" at the same time he castigates the executives of Teldar for lining their own pockets and for lazy mismanagement. He seduces Bud to greed while analysing the inequity of wealth in America. He's ostensibly using it as his justification for existence as a corporate shark, but it sounds more like a plea from a lone leftist activist.

Stone has said Bud is what he would have been had he followed in his father's footsteps, but the stockbroker father figure in this film isn't Bud's father, nor Gekko, but Lou Mannheim. Bud is a working-class boy on the make, believing in the dream; Stone was a disillusioned rich boy whose father was never made comfortable by privilege. Had Stone gone into the family business he would have been more like the Barnes character. In the end, though the film's dialectic is between Gekko and Mannheim, Bud's real choice is between Gekko and his real father.

Likewise, we know Gekko is doomed when we hear him using Vietnam language, "lock and load," in a Stone movie. Interesting too that Gekko's corporate bruiser, played for laughs by the unbruising Josh Mostel, is called Ollie.

*Wall Street* is also concerned with rising on the social scale, with buying one's way into Manhattan. It looks consciously to *The Great Gatsby* for inspiration. Gekko dresses in Redford-style Gatsby gear and calls Bud "sport." The Long Island beach scenes, including a sunrise straight out of Turner, recall Gatsby's setting. Gatsby, of course, was really Jay Gatz, an ethnic like Gekko and like Lou Stone (somehow I don't think Hal Holbrook's Lou Mannheim changed *his* name!).

Lou Mannheim drops pearls of wisdom like mini-Thumpers on Bud throughout the film. Lou says "money makes you do things you don't want to do," which is slightly less profound than, say, Danny De Vito's "everybody needs money, that's why they call it money!" in David Mamet's *Heist*. When Bud is arrested, Lou reminds him "man lives in the abyss…that's when a man finds his character," which would be more appropriate coming from Sergeant Elias rather than a stockbroker.

Another of the film's mantras is that making things is better than living off the production of others. Again, Stone creates a vivid metaphor for Hollywood where the rights of the money men to be identified as the creators of a motion picture are inviolate, and who gets arbitrated the credit is far more important than who actually does the work.

*The Real Lizard King:* Michael Douglas as the Wall Street lizard was an inspired bit of Stone casting against type; Douglas won the best actor Oscar and revitalised an acting career which had looked like giving way to his greater success as a producer. Douglas conveys both ruthlessness and weakness, particularly when matched against Terence Stamp's Wildman (yes, ironic, isn't it): the classic ethnic (read Jewish) vs. WASP confrontation. Douglas isn't necessarily the most convincing Jew, but Stone's take on WASPiness is interesting: "The English are a strict people…encrusted still with powerful repressed emotions of blame and guilt, a profoundly male judgmental culture." He claims to see many of the same characteristics in himself.

Gekko's moment of revelation and self-destruction actually comes when he stoops to attacking Bud Fox in the park, all the bullshit about *The Art Of War* forgotten. Still, for all Bud's redemption I'm sure the picture enticed more viewers to go into brokering than into aircraft maintenance.

Other casting is less successful, particularly Hannah as a successful decorator who "wants to do for furniture what Laura Ashley did for fabrics." Instead, she tries to do for movies what Cindy Crawford did. It's odd that powerful men find her so appealing, especially considering her taste in modern art; even odder that Gekko would have married Sean Young, whose backstory must've been more interesting that what we see. Strangely, Young bears a resemblance to the young Millie Perkins who has a small part as Bud's mother.

*On The Job Training:* The hooker with whom Gekko rewards Bud Fox is played by Andrea Thompson, who would finally graduate from soft-porn flicks to a starring role as the blouse-straining Detective Kirkendall on *NYPD Blue* before joining CNN as a newsreader, or—as they put it—an "experienced and talented journalist."

*The Thumper Wall Street:* gave birth to the mother of all thumpers: Gekko's "greed is good" speech is delivered as if he were a lawyer making closing arguments to a jury. The flattest line has to be Bud's "who am I?" as he stands on his balcony with Darryl Hannah waiting for him in bed.

*The Verdict:* Most of *Wall Street* makes more sense as a screenplay structure than it does as a logical film. Would Gekko be impressed with Bud Fox's espionage? Wouldn't he have private eyes standing by to do the same thing? Why is Wildman suddenly a good guy? Would Bud have gone through with the plan had Gekko only confided in him earlier? Would Bud really want a second date with Darryl Hannah? 3/5

## Talk Radio (1988)

*Cast:* Eric Bogosian (Barry Champlain), Alec Baldwin (Dan), Ellen Greene (Ellen), Leslie Hope (Laura), John C McGinley (Stu), John Pankow (Chuck Dietz), Michael Wincott (Kent), Robert Trebor (Jeffrey), Zach Grenier (Sid Greenberg), Tony Frank (Dino), Harlan Jordan (Coach Armstrong), Anna Levine (Drink-toss Woman), Bruno Rubeo (Terry), Rockets Redglare (Killer). *Voices include* Peter Zapp, Park Overall, Redglare (Redneck), Carl Kissin, Moby (Station Announcer/Newscaster), Earl Hindman (Chet/Black John/Jerry), Michele Mariana (Rhonda/Elderly Woman/Julia), Bill DeAcutis, Levine (Denise), Trebor.

*Crew:* Executive Producers: Greg Strangis, Sam Strangis; Producers: Edward R Pressman, A Kitman Ho (Universal/Cineplex Odeon/Pressman); Screenplay: Eric Bogosian, Stone, based on the play by Bogosian & Ted Savinar and the book *Talked To Death* by Stephen Singular; Photography: Robert Richardson; Camera Operator: Phil Pfeiffer; Aerial Photography: Jerry Callaway; Editor: David Brenner; Co-Editor: Joe Hutshing; Production Design: Bruno Rubeo; Music: Stewart Copeland; Production Manager: Clayton Townsend.

*Story:* Barry Champlain, host of KGAB Dallas' *Night Talk* call-in show, is offered Metrowave Radio national syndication. Uneasy at the possibility he might have to tone down his style leads him to ask his ex-wife Ellen to visit him for the weekend, without telling his girlfriend/producer Laura. He receives a death threat from a racist caller and is heckled at a local basketball game. In flashback we see suit salesman Barry get his break in radio and Ellen aiding him by playing 'Cheryl Ann', a caller. We also see Barry's ambition and his getting caught cheating on Ellen. He brings Ellen to the studio for his national broadcast but is told by Metrowave's Dietz that it is being delayed two weeks for 'corporate reasons'. Angry, Champlain invites a caller, stoned slacker Kent, to join him on the show. Station manager Dan threatens to fire him and Laura tells him not to blow both their chances. Barry overhears Ellen assuring her husband Lou she is only visiting Barry to "comfort a sick relative." Barry, stung by the perceived rejection, turns vicious. Kent remains oblivious to his insults but becomes hysterical with a suicidal caller and is kicked out. Ellen calls as Cheryl Ann and tells Barry she loves him; at the last instant he rejects her and she leaves the studio. Barry tells a racist caller he sees himself as a hypocrite and despises and fears his audience. Dan and Dietz think the show was great; Barry tells engineer Stu it was a wash-out and heads for Ellen's hotel to mend fences. He breaks up with Laura in the parking lot. On his way to his car he is stopped by an autograph hunter who kills him.

*Background:* Stone had originally been brought into the project as a possible co-producer by Ed Pressman who had optioned Eric Bogosian's play but wound up directing it while doing the pre-production for *Born On The Fourth Of July*. Stone's credentials as a Hollywood player were firmly established by this film deal; he and Pressman sold it to Cineplex Odeon for $10 million; it cost $4 million to make, so their profit was $3 million each.

Barry Champlain is such a prototype of Stone's angry, obsessed heroes that one is tempted to see it as a later, and better, self-portrait than Chris in *Platoon*. Barry becomes entranced with his radio career: his defining line comes during the flashback when his wife refuses to double as his producer because it might affect their marriage. "Fuck the marriage," he says, and means it. Barry also uses Vietnam twice as a defining moment, the second time to break up with his producer/girlfriend who, he says, doesn't remember Vietnam. She has earlier foreshadowed the flashback (!) by complaining that when she talks to him like a producer he treats her like a girlfriend and when she talks like a girlfriend he treats her like a wife. When we see his wife avoid the same sort of dilemma we know for sure (if we didn't know already) that their marriage is doomed.

Barry sees himself as a purveyor of issues, but station manager Dan remembers him when he was just "a suit salesman with big mouth." He asks if he really "thinks you are changing the world," something Stone has been accused many times of thinking he is doing. But as Barry says "I denounce the system as I embrace it," which is pretty much a perfect definition of Stone.

Barry also must make a decision between the responsibility of a 'family' who loves him (his ex-wife) and the job (his girlfriend is very much a part of the job to him and it is made clear a couple of times that he is just part of her career). In Stone, there is always the sense that the obsessive pursuit of any exterior goal is a sign not of self-awareness, as Gordon Gekko would have us believe, but of self-loathing.

Shock jocks were looked at as a new phenomenon at the time, though they were part of a tradition that went back to the rabble-rousing radio shows of Father Coughlin in the Thirties, and certainly to the late night galleries of the weird presented by such figures as Long John Nebel, Joe Pyne or Allen Burke in the early Sixties (the figures who inspired Donald Fagen's 'The Nightfly'). The difference was that no one took them serious politically.

Although Barry, like Alan Berg, the murdered Denver host on whom the story was based, appears to be a liberal, the majority of such performers are right-wing. Indeed, when he wraps himself in the Nazi flag a listener has sent, we get a sense of Stone's awareness of the fascist potential for any charismatic performer.

*True Love Ways:* Barry's Boyle-esque view of true love might best be expressed by a roach repellent ad the station broadcasts which begins with the sound of 'cockroaches mating'. His most personal moment comes when his ex-wife calls him up pretending to be Cheryl Ann; she reclines on a desk with the phone with a clear suggestion of intimacy. When we hear Barry told "you don't know how to love," and he is accused of self-loathing, we are hearing the same refrain that was directed at many Stone heroes from Boyle to Nixon and beyond. And just as Nixon is eventually summarised as a man who needed love, the political issues of *Talk Radio* morph into a question of whether or not Barry can choose to let himself be loved. He can't, and is killed as a result (would he be shot if he weren't alone getting into his car?).

*Open & Shut:* In opening out the story, Stone and Richardson play with reflections, move cameras around the studio and even give Barry a Madonna-mike years before radio stations did. As usual, Stone's insistence on realism makes the flashback extremely unsettling to watch: Bogosian's threads and wig would have been sick-making in their own time, much less 1988. The flashback detailing Barry and Ellen's backstory is Stone's main opening out of the original play and provides a necessary plot point (Ellen's Cheryl Ann character), but it never really feels integrated.

*The Thumper:* Champlain's confession to the audience: "I'm a hypocrite...I ask for sincerity and I lie...the world is a terrible place...everybody's screwed up and you like it that way," has the tone of the lectures tacked onto the end of Thirties gangster movies which, after showing you how cool gangsters were, warned you that crime doesn't pay. Barry then explains to the audience who they actually are. It is followed, of course, by his loving producer telling him she doesn't think he is the bad guy he thinks he is. Then he dies.

*The Verdict:* There is a lot to like about *Talk Radio* and it moves with an intensity that at times makes you feel like you're watching a 'real time' movie. There are a couple of badly misjudged moments, including the sound of a gas oven as Barry lights a cigarette while a caller denies the Holocaust. Barry's public persona seems so amorphous it's hard to figure out why the redneck callers are so incensed politically; he's an asshole on the air, but his politics veer as much to the right as to the left. This is where Stone's sense of the personal rather than the political driving his stories is most obvious. There's a fine supporting performance by Baldwin and, in passing, Michael Wincott's Kent, although seemingly too old to be who he is, invents the voices of Beavis and Butthead. It also loses points for its coda, another mini-Thumper which is unnecessary unless you feel the audience hasn't been listening. 3/5

# 8: The Vietnam Trilogy

Stone's Vietnam films are his most honoured. *Platoon* was nominated for eight Oscars and won four (Best Picture, Director, Editing and Sound). It had also taken the first two categories at the Golden Globes (along with a best supporting actor prize for Tom Berenger) and won the DGA and BAFTA best director nods.

Three years later, he would win the best director Oscar again for his next Vietnam film, *Born On The Fourth Of July* and, again, his editors would be honoured, although the best picture award went to the more upbeat *Driving Miss Daisy*. Tom Cruise's performance as Ron Kovic—surely his best ever—lost the Oscar battle of the disabled to Daniel Day-Lewis in *My Left Foot*.

By the time Stone made *Heaven And Earth*, *JFK* had altered some perceptions of him; he was held to far harsher critical standards. The film, which completed a trilogy of three views (the war itself, the American home front and the battle-stricken Vietnam), was also a far different proposition for Stone. Not only was it his first (and only film to date) to tell a woman's story, it also flopped at the box office unlike the highly successful earlier films set in that predominantly male universe.

## Platoon (1986)

*Cast:* Tom Berenger (Sgt. Barnes), Willem Dafoe (Sgt. Elias), Charlie Sheen (Chris Taylor), Keith David (King), Forest Whitaker (Big Harold), John McGinley (Sgt. O'Neill), Kevin Dillon (Bunny), Reggie Johnson (Junior), Francesco Quinn (Rhah), Corey Glover (Francis), Mark Moses (Lt. Wolfe), Dale Dye (Captain Harris), Richard Edson (Sal), Johnny Depp (Lerner), Corkey Ford (Manny), David Neidorf (Tex), Bob Orwig (Gardner), Chris Pedersen (Crawford), J Adam Glover (Sandy), Stone (Battalion Commander).

*Crew:* Executive Producers: John Daly, Derek Gibson; Producer: Arnold Kopelson (Orion/Hemdale); Co-Producer: A Kitman Ho; Screenplay: Stone; Photography: Robert Richardson; Assistant DP: Chris Lombardi; Additional Photography: Georges Rosales, Caloy Salcedo; Editor: Claire Simpson; Music: Georges Delerue; Second Unit Photography: Tom Sigel; Production Design: Bruno Rubeo; Special Effects & Visual Continuity: Gordon J Smith; Stunt Coordinator: Gil Arceoa; Military Advisor: Dale Dye.

*Story:* Chris Taylor arrives in Vietnam in 1967. Sent out within days by battle-scarred Sgt. Barnes—over the objections of Sgt. Elias—Taylor is wounded and fellow 'cherry' Gardner is killed when Junior falls asleep on watch; but Junior shifts the blame to Taylor. Returning to the unit, Taylor reveals to King he is a college drop-out who volunteered for Vietnam. He discovers the unit is divided between 'heads' and 'rednecks', he becomes part of the former group, getting high with Elias. On patrol, they discover a Vietcong bunker; booby traps kill two soldiers and the VC get a third. In the nearby village, a disturbed Taylor uses his gun to make a retarded Vietnamese boy dance; Bunny then clubs him to death. Barnes, interrogating the village chief, shoots his wife and threatens his daughter before Elias intervenes; they fight. They torch the village and Taylor stops three soldiers raping a Vietnamese girl. Elias reports Barnes to Captain Harris who makes harsh noises but takes no action because he needs soldiers in the field. The next day, King is sent home three days early. As battle begins, Lt. Wolfe calls in the wrong co-ordinates for artillery fire and several of his men are killed; Barnes forcibly stops the officer. Elias has taken Taylor and two others to cut off the VC and prevent them from catching B company in a cross-fire; he leaves the other three to do the same to the VC. While he is gone, Barnes orders Wolfe to withdraw, leaving Elias' men isolated, and then orders Taylor and the others back while saying he will find Elias who, meanwhile, has cut a swath through the VC. Barnes shoots Elias; then tells Taylor that Elias has been killed. As the platoon is evacuated, Taylor sees Elias chased down by the VC and killed. Back at base he fights with Barnes, who nearly kills him. Near the Cambodian border, they are being overrun by the North Vietnamese regulars when Captain Harris orders a napalm strike over his own position. The napalm hits just as Barnes is about to kill Taylor. Waking, Taylor finds Barnes badly wounded and, picking up a Vietnamese AK47, kills him. Junior wounds himself. Both are choppered off the battlefield and, by implication, out of Vietnam.

*Background:* The film that established Stone as a major player and defined his post-*Scarface*, pre-*JFK* image, *Platoon* remains a vivid portrayal of the chaos of war and a realistic-seeming look into the mindsets of the American soldiers on the ground. Having adapted a political story into a personal one in *Salvador*, Stone repeated the feat but, because it reflects his own experiences so clearly, it is even more intensely personal. The same critics who disliked the perceived radical politics of *Salvador* were quick to jump on *Platoon*'s ignoring of political issues. The Vietnam war fought in *Platoon* is in many ways the same one fought in *The Deer Hunter* or *Coming Home,* less a war against Vietnamese than a battle for America's soul. Where it differs is that the battle is played out in the combat zone and reduced symbolically to the struggle between Sergeants Elias and Barnes for the heart and mind of Chris Taylor. The Vietnamese have a presence resembling, say, the role of Indians in John Ford's *Fort Apache*: the enemy are presented with respect but they are not really relevant to the major conflict of the story which is within the souls of American soldiers.

Those soldiers are American innocents, capable of torching a village, murdering and raping, and then carrying the small children out in their arms. The scene is one of Stone's best at catching that paradox.

*Platoon* is the story of a young man's coming of age in warfare and, like most Stone heroes, Chris Taylor must learn to face the beast within him. To make *Platoon*, Stone had his actors put through a mini-boot camp run by military advisor Dale Dye, who not only plays in this film and other Stone pictures as a very useful character actor but went on to become Hollywood's favourite soldier, serving most recently as a technical advisor on the HBO television series *Band Of Brothers*. Stone would repeat the experience in many of his films, running a football camp before *Any Given Sunday* or having Joan Chen work in rice paddies before *Heaven And Earth*.

Stone's own Vietnam experience introduced him to both rock music in general and black music and culture in particular and the importance of bridging the racial gap is crucial to the film, as it would be in *Any Given Sunday*. *Platoon* marked the beginning of a changing attitude toward the war movie. Stone brought the focus of the war film back into the foxholes after Vietnam had rendered the old-fashioned paean to patriotism obsolete. It's fair to say that *Platoon* provided the template for Spielberg's *Saving Private Ryan* and *Band Of Brothers* where heroism is defined as dying not for your country but for your buddies. The difference, for Stone, is that, based on his own experience, heroism is merely a moment of surrender to the beast that lurks within. This is how he has described his own actions when he won the Bronze Star and it is what defines Taylor's bravery in the film's final firefight. Taylor surrenders to the Sgt. Barnes within him because the zen-master approach of Sgt. Elias isn't enough. But he then kills Barnes, avenges Elias and, in effect, silences the beast within himself. At least until he gets to Hollywood.

If Charlie Sheen's killing of Barnes doesn't carry the mythological load of Martin Sheen's ritual murder of Kurtz in *Apocalypse Now* (the casting of Sheen must encourage the connection), Elias' death certainly loads it back on.

*The Thumper:* Taylor's final voice-over sums up all the points, in case you missed them first time around: "We did not fight the enemy, we fought ourselves and the enemy was us…I was a child born of two fathers…Elias and Barnes were fighting for my soul."

*The Verdict: Platoon's* battle scenes stand up, though the heavy-handed symbolism in Elias' death still grates, and Taylor's Thumper conclusion dilutes the whole effect. Still, 4/5.

## Born On The Fourth Of July (1989)

*Cast:* Tom Cruise (Ron Kovic), Carolina Kava (Mrs Kovic), Raymond J Barry (Mr Kovic), Bryan Larkin (young Ron), Josh Evans (Tommy Kovic), Seth Allen (Young Tommy), Jamie Talisman (Jimmy Kovic), Sean Stone (young Jimmy), Anne Bobby (Suzanne Kovic), Jenna Van Oy (Young Suzanne), Samantha Larkin (Patty Kovic), Erika Geminder (Young Patty), Kevin Harvey Morse (Jackie). *Massapequa*: Kyra Sedgwick (Donna), Jessica Prunell (Young Donna), Frank Whaley (Timmy), Jason Klein (Young Timmy), Jerry Levine (Steve), Lane Davis (Young Steve), Richard Panebianco (Joey), John Pinto (Young Joey), Rob Camilletti (Tommy), J R Nutt (Young Tommy), Stephen Baldwin (Billy), Philip Amelio (Young Billy), Michael McTighe (Danny), Cody Beard (Young Danny), Ryan Beadle (Ballplayer), Harold Woloschin (Umpire), Richard Grusin (Coach), Tom Berenger (Recruiting Sergeant), Richard Haus (Second Sergeant), Mel Allen (Himself), Ed Lauter (Legion Commander), Liz Moore (Fat Lady), Sean McGraw (Young Donna's father), Stone (News Reporter), Dale Dye (Colonel), Norma Moore (Mom), Stacey Moseley (Young Donna's Friend). *Vietnam*: John Getz (Major), David Warshofsky (Lieutenant), Jason Gedrick (Martinez), Michael Compotaro (Wilson), Platoon includes: William Baldwin, James LeGros, William Mapother, Markus Flanagan (Doctor), R D Call (Chaplain). *Veteran's Hospital*: Corky Ford (Marvin), Rocky Carroll (Willie), Willie Minor (Eddie), Billie Neal (Nurse Washington), Richard Poe (Frankie), Vivica Fox (Hooker), Mark Moses (Doctor). *Syracuse*: Abbie Hoffman (Strike Organiser), Jake Weber (Donna's Boyfriend), Edie Brickell (Folksinger), Joseph Reidy (Student Organiser). *Arthur's Bar*: Holly Marie Combs (Jenny), Melina Ramos Renner (Barmaid), Mike Starr, Beau Starr, Rick Masters (Men). *Villa Dulce*: Willem Dafoe (Charlie), Tom Sizemore, Andrew Lauer, Michael Wincott (Vets), Cordelia González (Maria Elena), Karen Newman (Whore), Begonia Plaza (Charlie's Whore), Edith Diaz (Madam), Anthony Pena (Bartender), Eduardo Ricardo (Cabbie). *Georgia*: Tony Frank (Mr Wilson), Jayne Haynes (Mrs Wilson), Lili Taylor (Jamie Wilson), Elbert Lewis (Cabbie). *Miami*: Peter Crombie (Undercover Vet), Chuck Pfeiffer (Secret Service Agent), Chip Moody (TV Anchor), Frank Girardeau, William Wallace (Agents), Kevin McGuire, Ken Osborne, Alan Toy (Paraplegics), Eagle Eye Cherry, Brian Tarantina, Frank Cavestani, Jimmy Parker (Vets), William Knight (Chief), David Carriere

(Hippie), John Galt (Fat Republican). *Democratic Convention*: Jack McGee (Delegate), Daniel Baldwin (Vet), Jodi Long, Michelle Hurst (Reporters) Annie McEnroe, Elizabeth Hoffman, Keri Roebuck.

*Crew:* Producers: A Kitman Ho, Stone (Universal/Ixtlan), Jose V Luban Jr. (Philippines); Associate Producers: Clayton Townsend, Joseph Reidy; Screenplay: Stone, Ron Kovic, based on the book by Kovic; Photography: Robert Richardson; Camera Operator: Philip Pfeiffer; Editor: David Brenner, Co-Editor: Philip Hutshing; Music: John Williams; Production Design: Bruno Rubeo; Art Directors: Victor Kempster, Richard Johnson, Rodell Cruz (Philippines); Stunt Coordinator (Philippines): Gil Arceo.

*Story:* Ron Kovic grows up a true believer in the American way in Fifties and Sixties Long Island. Disappointed after losing a key wrestling match, he enlists in the Marines after hearing the challenge from a recruiting sergeant. On the eve of his departure, he runs through the rain to have the last dance at the prom with his girl Donna. In Vietnam, on his second tour, his unit attacks a village which contains only old people and children, but they are ambushed by the North Vietnamese. In the confusion Kovic thinks he may have killed Wilson, a new arrival. He decides he did and tries to report this, but the officer refuses to acknowledge his confession. On his next patrol, Ron is wounded, his spine severed. He ends up paralysed from the waist down. He is sent to a veterans' hospital where conditions are horrible and he is ignored. He returns home in a wheelchair and is guest of honour at a 4th of July parade which is disrupted by anti-war protesters. His brother is anti-war, as is Donna, now a student at Syracuse with a boyfriend. When Ron visits, he is caught in a strike demonstration protesting the invasion of Cambodia and hassled by the police. At home, he increasingly thinks of himself self-pityingly as a freak, hangs out in bars and frightens his pious mother when she confronts him, angrily describing his now-useless penis. He leaves for Mexico where he discovers other Vietnam paraplegics living a life of debauched excess. He enjoys it for a while, but eventually the frustration builds and after a fight with his mentor, Charlie, he leaves. Travelling to Georgia to apologise to Wilson's family, he receives some solace from them. He joins the Veterans against the War and demonstrates at the 1972 Republican convention in Miami. After writing a book, he addresses the 1976 Democratic convention from the platform, rejoining American society. In a voice-over, we hear his mother's recollected dream of his speaking before a large important group, a dream originally prompted by John Kennedy's inaugural speech in 1961.

*Background:* The success of *Platoon* proved there was life beyond *Rambo* and Stone was able to make *Born On The Fourth Of July* ten years after his attempt with Al Pacino had fallen by the wayside. Tom Cruise, himself born on July 3, fell in love with the script and the role and Cruise's participation got the film made. "I could feel the script in my balls," he said. Ironically, Cruise was coming off a huge success in *Top Gun*, a post-Vietnam film very much on the *Rambo* end of the spectrum. If anything, the resonance of Cruise's fairy-tale heroics in the earlier film added to the power of *Born On The Fourth Of July*. Certainly Stone's reputation as someone willing to cast against type and as a director able to elicit performances from actors was cemented by Cruise, who was inexplicably passed over for the Oscar.

When we think of the young, conservative Stone volunteering for Vietnam to, in effect, find himself, we can see the germ of Ron Kovic's disillusionment with everything the 4th of July stands for. This film presents Kovic as a sucker for believing to a far greater degree than Chris Taylor: Chris learns that it's a war fought to benefit the rich while Kovic learns that all the John Wayne myths are false. Because he has bought into the myths so desperately (to compensate, it is implied, for his failures at wrestling and with his girl), his psychological fall is as devastating as his physical one.

Kovic is also, like Boyle, searching for redemption. Boyle finds his in Salvador, only to lose it when he comes home; Kovic loses his faith first in Vietnam and, on his return to America, has it completely destroyed. He tries going south of the Border, looking for salvation in drugs and sex, but it doesn't work and he must make peace, literally, with America before he can be saved. He makes this peace through mainstream political action, a premise which shows how misplaced Stone's radical reputation essentially is.

*The Thumper:* There are thumpers galore, including Ron's savage indictment thrown at the security men throwing him out of the Republican convention. His simple "It's been a long way for us...and just lately I've felt like I'm home," never loses its overtones of *The Wizard Of Oz* for me.

*The Verdict:* This has moments of extreme emotional impact where the feelings of all sides of Stone's generation are laid out plainly. It's easily the finest performance of Cruise's career and I don't say that with the perennial Oscar bias toward people playing characters with disabilities. But the whole thing comes at you with steamroller subtlety and the intensity at times just can't be maintained. 3/5

# Heaven And Earth (1993)

*Cast:* Hiep Thi Le (Le Ly), Tommy Lee Jones (Steve Butler), Joan Chen (Mama), Haing S Ngor (Papa), Lan Nguyen Calderon (Ba), Thuan Le (Kim), Dustin Nguyen (Bon), Debbie Reynolds (Eugenia Butler), Conchata Ferrell (Bernice), Long Nguyen (Anh Lien), Vivian Wu (Madame Lien), Timothy Carhart (Big Mike), Dale Dye (Larry), Le Ly Hayslip (Jewellery Broker).

*Crew:* Executive Producer: Mario Kaiser; Producers: Stone, Argon Milton, Robert Kiln, A Kitman Ho (Warner Bros./Regency); Co-Producer: Clayton Townsend; Screenplay: Stone, based on the books *When Heaven And Earth Changed Places* by Le Ly Hayslip with Jay Wurts and *Child Of War, Woman Of Peace* by Le Ly Hayslip with James Hayslip; Photography: Robert Richardson; Second Unit DP: Philip Pfeiffer; Editors: David Brenner, Sally Menke; Production Design: Victor Kempster; Music: Kitaro; Musical Director/Orchestrations: Randy Miller.

*Story:* Le Ly grows up in an idyllic Vietnamese village, scarcely bothered by the war against the French. When the Vietcong arrive to fight against the partition of the country, her two brothers go off to fight. Government troops move in and re-education begins but Le Ly, like most of the village, secretly helps the VC. She is arrested and tortured by government soldiers with US advisors. Her mother bribes an official to get her released but in her village everyone assumes she has collaborated. About to be executed by the VC, she is raped by the soldiers assigned to kill her. Shamed, her mother takes her to Saigon where they join the domestic staff of a wealthy Catholic, Anh Lien. He seduces her; she becomes pregnant and is sent to Danang where his support is soon cut off and she supports herself selling black-market goods to soldiers and picking garbage. She tries to avoid prostitution, though eventually she succumbs at least once to a big money offer from a friendly sergeant, Big Mike, pimping for two 'short-timers'.

After returning to her village, where her father tells her to do the best she can for her son, she goes back to Danang, getting a job as a waitress in a servicemen's bar. Sergeant Steve Butler arranges to meet her and eventually convinces her he is not after "boom boom." They become lovers, having a son. As Saigon comes close to falling they are separated, but he finds her and they marry. He brings her back to San Diego where she meets his family and finds it hard to adjust to the abundance and waste of America as well as the tacit racism she encounters. Steve is under pressure from his ex-wife for alimony payments but forbids Le Ly to work and explodes when he discovers she has been working in secret. He reveals that he has no prospects of a civilian career because he has been a 'black ops' assassin in Vietnam. His behaviour becomes more abusive and when Le Ly seeks a divorce, he kidnaps the kids. She agrees to reconcile but he kills himself. Thirteen years later, Le Ly, now a successful American businesswoman, takes her children back to Vietnam. Her eldest meets his father, now a street vendor. They return to her village where her brother is resentful of her life in the land of their enemy. But her mother blames herself for forcing her other son to go to war and die and welcomes Le Ly back saying she is proud of her success. With the return to her village, Le Ly puts the spirit of her father to rest.

*Background:* The third of Stone's Vietnam films is his least personal and most concerned with setting records straight and covering all the bases. It might be seen as an inverse of *Born On The Fourth Of July*. It is one of the few American films to examine the Vietnam experience from the point of view of the Vietnamese, admitting that the war was not fought entirely in the conscience of America but in the countryside of Vietnam, portrayed here as an idyllic paradise as beautiful as Spike Lee's Brooklyn.

Le Ly is yet another Stone character forced to choose between parental drives, in this case her father's desire for her to stay close to the land and her mother's insistence, after her rape, that she leave and find her way in the world. This somewhat inverts the traditional Buddhist paradigm of father Heaven and mother Earth, showing, as the voice-over acknowledges at the film's end when Le Ly tells us the moral of the story, that she has been caught between both; it reminds us of Stone's own precarious perch between the work ethic of his father and the wildness of his mother, to whom the film is dedicated.

Having accepted her mother's suggestion to surrender to shame and leave her village, Le Ly must later choose again, between Vietnam and America. Since both VC and ARVN soldiers torture her as a traitor, it is not just Americans who abuse Vietnamese women.

This is Stone's first film with a female lead and is structured very much in the 'survivor' mode of an Oprah Winfrey heroine (Stone would be executive producer of *The Joy Luck Club*, also in 1993). But Le Ly's story is really one of the various men who dominate her life and her efforts to come to peace with disappointing her father's expectations. One of the movie's best scenes shows her father waiting for Le Ly outside the bedroom where her older sister Kim entertains a GI client. Le Ly hides down the hall, embarrassed because she is pregnant by Lien.

Joan Chen, who played the mother, originally wanted the part of Le Ly but was turned down, probably because she would have had trouble playing the young girl (although usually Stone is not averse to using multiple actors to show stages in a character's development). It's hard not to think that he preferred to cast Hiep, a student with no acting experience, precisely for the helplessness she would project playing against experienced actors.

There is also an element of male voyeuristic pleasure in the rape scene, which included prosthetic breasts for Hiep (who was uneasy about baring her own), while the love scene between Hiep and Jones comes off as Emmanuelle in Danang. The film is not helped by the slushy score by Kitaro, itself made worse by overdone orchestrations which gall throughout. But the basic difficulty with the film is that the main character remains ultimately acted upon, rather than acting. We never see the change in Le Ly, from Asian wife (the virtues of which are elaborated, discomfortingly, by Dale Dye in the Thanksgiving dinner scene) to American entrepreneuse; she strikes out on her own and we next see her when she has returned to her child rôle to see her mother again.

*The Thumper:* Although there is a sub-thumper ("different skin, same suffering") the real one lies in wait at the end. "You have completed your cycle of growth—the past is now complete and my destiny as your mother is now over." "It is my fate to be between heaven and earth, we need only once correct our mistakes."

*The Verdict:* Although there is much to like in this film, too much of it retains Stone's macho melodramatic feel to really settle down to Le Ly's story, which remains incomplete. 2/5

# 9: The Sixties Trilogy

These films, made consecutively with only the interruption of *Heaven And Earth*, are all historical dramas which reflect the closeness of Vietnam to the Sixties experience without using war scenes. Vietnam is present in the background throughout *The Doors*, whose music is now inextricably associated with Vietnam movies anyway; the war provides the central motivation for the murder of John Kennedy in *JFK*; and the echoes of that murder are the chilling secret at the heart of *Nixon*. Between the indulgence of *The Doors* and the worthiness of *Heaven And Earth*, Stone showed just how far he'd progressed from Stanley Kramer, turning out two historical epics full of high-profile casts in bit parts that both entertained and inspired profound debate. Kramer plus Scorsese indeed. These three films brought together everything Stone had learned about film-making. He began to expand his shooting to include multiple stocks, speeds and formats. His editing gained in intensity, as if he realised that history and the appearance of straightforward ideas required something more to keep it entertaining. Remember there had been few successful rock bio-films.

## The Doors (1991)

*Cast:* Val Kilmer (Jim Morrison), Meg Ryan (Pam Courson), Kyle MacLachlan (Ray Manzarek), Frank Whaley (Robby Krieger), Kevin Dillon (John Densmore), Kathleen Quinlan (Patricia Kennealy), Michael Madsen (Tom Baker), Michael Wincott (Paul Rothchild), Dennis Burkley (Dog), Crispin Glover (Andy Warhol), Josh Evans (Bill Siddons), Billy Idol (Cat), Mimi Rogers (Photographer), Jennifer Rubin (Edie Sedgewick), Kristina Fulton (Nico), Paul Williams (Warhol PR), Michael Wincott (Paul Rothschild), John Densmore (Engineer, last session), Kelly Ann Hu (Dorothy), Josie Bisset (Rob's Girlfriend), Debbie Falconer (John's Girl), Floyd Red Crow Westerman (Shaman), Wes Studi, Rion Hunter, Steve Reevis (Indians in desert), Gretchen Becker (Mom), Jerry Sturm (Dad), Sean Stone (Young Jim), Kendall Deichen (Sister), Mark Moses (Jac Holzman), Bob Lupone (Manager), Paul Rothchild (Manager's Sidekick), Michele Bronson (NY Groupie), Will Jordan (Ed Sullivan), Sam Whipple (CBS Producer), Charlie Spradling (CBS Girl backstage), Lisa Edelstein (Make-up Artist), Costas Mandylor (Italian Count), Bill Graham (New Haven Promoter), Titus Welliver (Cop with mace), Eagle Eye Cherry, David Allen Brooks (Roadies), Bonnie Bramlett (Bartender), Hawthorne James (Chuck Vincent), Alan Manson (Judge), William Kunstler (Lawyer), Bob Marshall

(Prosecutor), Annie McEnroe (Secretary), Kelly Leach (Birthday Girl), uncredited: Oliver Stone (Film Teacher).

*Crew:* Producers: Bill Graham, Sasha Harari, A Kitman Ho (Tri-Star/ Carolco); Executive Producers: Mario Kassar, Nicholas Clainos, Brian Grazer; Screenplay: J Randal Johnson, Stone; Photography: Robert Richardson; Editors: David Brenner, Joe Hutshing; Production Design: Barbara Ling; Music Producer: Paul Rothchild; Executive Music Producer: Budd Carr; Second Unit Camera: Tom Sigel, Toby Phillips.

*Story:* A fat, bearded Jim Morrison reads his poetry at a solo recording session. Moving west to California, the Morrison family encounter a group of Indians, victims of a car crash in the desert. In 1967, Jim Morrison follows Pamela Courson home from Venice Beach. He drops out of UCLA film school, discouraged by criticism of his student film. On the beach he re-encounters fellow student Ray Manzarek who is impressed with Jim's poetry; they put together a band and begin playing the LA scene. Jim is offered the chance to go solo but the group takes decisions collectively, like the Three Musketeers. At the Whisky a Go Go, LA's top venue, Morrison's performance goes over the top but impresses producer Paul Rothchild who signs them to Jac Holzman's Elektra Records. Jim takes the band into the desert to have mystical experiences on acid. They perform in San Francisco and shock the Ed Sullivan show by saying "higher" in violation of network standards and practices. While in New York, they are taken to meet Andy Warhol and Pam catches Nico going down on Jim. After an unsuccessful press conference, Jim seduces journalist Patricia Kennealy who is also a witch. To try and make Jim jealous, Pam is caught in bed doing heroin with an Italian count hanger-on of Warhol's. When New Haven police mace Jim after catching him with Patricia in the men's room he starts a riot; the police break up the show. Back in California, a Thanksgiving party ends in a jealous fight with Pam when Patricia shows up. Morrison's drinking and drug taking upset the balance of the band; Jim is revolted to discover the others have sold the tune of 'Light My Fire' for car adverts. Jim is convicted of indecency in Miami after exposing himself on stage while being contemptuous of his fans. Patricia tells him she is pregnant but he wants nothing to do with a child. Pam talks him in after he goes on the roof of the Chateau Marmont to commit suicide. With The Doors finished as a group, Jim patches things up with the rest of the band and goes to Paris with Pam. He is found dead in his bath from an apparent heart attack, according to the closing titles, and is buried in Père Lachaise cemetery.

*Background: The Doors* was made, in the end, without the co-operation of Ray Manzarek, their keyboard player, and with very tough strings attached by the family of Pam Courson. At $38 million it was Stone's most expensive picture to date and took two months to shoot. Stone managed to recreate actual concerts, shooting them documentary-style and encouraging his 3,000 extras to indulge like it was Woodstock recreated.

The project had been years in development, with directors as diverse as Brian De Palma, Paul Schrader, Walter Hill and Ron Howard attached, and with an even more amazing array of actors considered, from Timothy Bottoms to John Travolta. Columbia Pictures had acquired the rights in the mid-Eighties and Stone had been considered as a scriptwriter. When Imagine bought the picture from Columbia, Stone met with the group, who had script approval, but they rejected him. By the time Andrew Vadja at Carolco came on board in 1989, Stone had done *Platoon* and when he was suggested as director the group agreed. Stone was originally scheduled to start as soon as he finished directing *Evita* which, of course, didn't happen.

Columbia's original research and script had been done by Randal Johnson. After so long in turnaround, Johnson needed to go to arbitration to get a share of the writing credit on the finished product. As the story goes, he attended the opening night with a Columbia executive, spotted Stone at the back of the theatre and introduced himself saying, "Hello, Oliver, I'm your co-writer."

*Before You Slip IntoUnconsciousness:* One of the amazing things about this film is the way it manages to convey the sense of self-indulgence which lay at the heart of the Sixties. It does it so well you often feel like you're coming down from a trip and distracted by a bad case of the munchies when you should be paying attention. On the other hand, the power of the concert scenes—surely the best ever staged—makes me stop and wonder. Were we really like that?

To many people The Doors weren't that big a thing, mostly because, once you got past their great early moments and reached their musical repetition phase and Morrison's adolescent poetry, a little turned out to go a very long way, which is why the extended "Light My Fire" is so compelling. If you didn't need to discover a Dionysian role model in Jim Morrison, The Doors weren't a defining moment for you, much less for your generation. To Stone, discovering The Doors as a grunt in Vietnam, the music is secondary to Morrison as a figure of liberation and his Dionysian stature is, of course, increased by his decline into a life of waste and excess. He serves exactly the kind of purpose that Elvis did for the blue-collar youth born before World War II. The Sixties kids were baby boomers, but most of their own cultural icons were, like Stone, older children born during World War II. Stone, thus, becomes a child of two wars; the importance of Morrison to Vietnam movies is evident to anyone who remembers the opening scene of *Apocalypse Now*. The contrast of the two directors' use of the song "The

End" is interesting: for Coppola the song is about nihilism; for Stone the key moment is Morrison's scream of Oedipal lust, a theme he visited in his novel.

Morrison is the patron saint of spiritual indulgence. Research on the film included Robert Richardson's mushroom trip to 'see' exactly what Morrison's desert would have looked like in his own mind. Stone and Rutkowski chartered a jet to attend a peyote festival in the Dakotas and charged it to the film's research budget. These were only the most immediate sign of the influence of Morrison's lifestyle on him. Like most Stone heroes, Morrison is forced to choose between his parents' world (Morrison's father was actually a US Navy officer deeply involved in the Gulf of Tonkin affair) and the world of his obsession; he appears to make this choice early, when he views the Indian car wreck in the desert and his mother tells him it is all a dream.

Later, Morrison will have another Stone choice presented to him, between his pure-in-spirit blonde muse, Pam, and the dark-haired devil woman, Patricia. This is first presented in genre fashion, something Stone will do in each of the Sixties films. *The Doors*, like many of Stone's films, can be read as a horror picture as Jim Morrison becomes possessed by Patricia, the reincarnation of Martine Beswick's Queen of Evil, and by the Warhol Factory crowd, who are referred to specifically as "vampires." The artist's dilemma is presented clearly. Pam, in her key scene, is a homemaker preparing Thanksgiving dinner and goes ballistic when 'the whore' shows up.

But she can't offer Jim the black magic his art demands. As if to stack the deck, even Pam's own drug use is shown primarily as a way of getting back at Jim (and being administered to her by a man as if she can't do it herself). When Jim chooses black magic bad things happen (he is maced by police in New Haven simply because he is talking to her), while Pam can save him from bad things (she talks him out of a suicide jump). Morrison will also reject Pat once she turns motherly (literally, telling him she is going to have a baby).

It's hard not to see some of Stone's own marriage in the Morrisons. Pam may be his muse but she introduces herself as an ornament. What is important to Stone is the way the tortured artist has to drive himself, ride the snake, and must inevitably prove unworthy of his muse's love (or, if he subsumes his art to her demands and goes to Paris, must die). One man's trip is another man's bummer.

We can see a lot of Jim Morrison in Stone's own film-making. The Doors were a group (the film notes Krieger wrote 'Light My Fire') whose core was the interplay of Morrison's voice and sexuality playing off against the coolness of Manzarek's swirling organ. As Morrison drifted more into himself, the group suffered, though Stone sees his later work as more impressive. But the analogy to film-making is clear and the Stone/Richardson partnership often suggests hints of the Morrison/Manzarek.

*I Love Paris In The Strung-Out Time:* Ironically, Stone had once gone to Paris to kick his own drug habit. Morrison's actual cause of death in Paris, which the film slides past, is generally believed to have been from a heroin overdose.

*Bit Parts:* Original Door John Densmore plays the engineer at Morrison's final recording sessions; Doors' producer Paul Rothchild has a part as well. Rocker Bonnie Bramlett (Delany and Bonnie) is the bartender in the biker bar and a warning to us all about what happens to rockers who don't die young. But the most interesting bit is an uncredited appearance by Stone as Morrison's film teacher at UCLA. Done up with a beard to resemble Martin Scorsese, Stone gets overpowered by the class' reaction to Morrison's pretentious student film.

*The Thumper:* It really isn't Morrison's reading poetry into the tape machine, though if it is it is the least thumpy of them all (note that a tape machine stopping is the final shot of *Talk Radio*). It's probably a fat Morrison being asked what he's going to do when the music's over (turn out the lights, as it turns out).

*The Verdict:* Films about rock music have been notoriously unsuccessful, although concert movies are the exception. So it's no surprise that Stone's concert scenes are brilliant, as good as any real concert. The *Star Is Born* progression of the rock band, although a cliché, has some elements of life breathed into it. On the other hand, the indulgence of Morrison and the era are replicated too faithfully, meaning much of the movie slows down to the boring level. And Meg Ryan never really looks like she likes what she's doing. 2/5

# JFK (1991)

*Cast:* Kevin Costner (Jim Garrison), Gary Oldman (Lee Harvey Oswald), Sissy Spacek (Liz Garrison), Tommy Lee Jones (Clay Shaw), Joe Pesci (David Ferrie), Donald Sutherland (Colonel X), Laurie Metcalf (Susie Cox), Michael Rooker (Bill Broussard), Jay O Sanders (Lou Ivon), Wayne Knight (Numa), Sally Kirkland (Rose Cheramie), Walter Matthau (Senator Russell Long), Ed Asner (Guy Bannister), Jack Lemmon (Jack Martin), Tony Plana (Carlos Bringuier), John Candy (Dean Andrews), Kevin Bacon (Willie O'Keefe), Vincent D'Onofrio (Bill Newman), Pruitt Taylor Vince (Lee Bowers), Brian Doyle-Murray (Jack Ruby), Beata Pozniak (Marina

Oswald), Jo Anderson (Julia Ann Mercer), Sean Stone (Jasper), uncredited: Frank Whaley (Second Oswald), Lolita Davidovich (Beverly Oliver).

*Crew:* Executive Producer: Arnon Milchan; Producers: A Kitman Ho, Stone (Warner Bros.); Co-Producer: Clayton Townsend; Screenplay: Stone, Zachary Sklar, based on *On The Trail Of The Assassins* by Jim Garrison and *Crossfire* by Jim Marrs; Photography: Robert Richardson; Camera Operator: Philip Pfeiffer; Editors: Joe Hutshing, Pietro Scalia, Hank Corwin; Production Design: Victor Kempster; Music: John Williams; Narration: Martin Sheen.

*Story:* A voice-over narration sets the scene for the Kennedy 'Camelot', including Dwight Eisenhower's warning about the 'military industrial complex'. Rose Cheramie, a drug addict hooker is dumped on a highway; in hospital she warns that Kennedy is about to be assassinated. JFK, meanwhile, is landing in Dallas.

News of the assassination reaches New Orleans DA Jim Garrison who goes to a local bar to watch TV coverage. In a dingier bar, private eye Guy Bannister celebrates while on TV Oswald denies his guilt. Bannister, drunk and paranoid, pistol-whips his friend Jack Martin, who recalls Oswald from Bannister's offices the past summer. Oswald is killed by Jack Ruby. Garrison interviews David Ferrie, an oddball pilot. The FBI immediately announce Ferrie is cleared of any suspicion. Three years later, Senator Russell Long tells Garrison he doesn't believe the Warren Report. Garrison begins to study the 26-volume report and discovers that Oswald, a purported Communist, had close ties to Bannister and intelligence types in New Orleans. Jack Martin says Oswald was involved in their operations to arm Cuban exiles. Local lawyer Dean Andrews told the Warren Commission one 'Clay Bertrand' had asked him to defend Oswald but tells Garrison he won't identify Bertrand. Convict Willie O'Keefe claims he was hired as a gay prostitute by Bertrand who was involved with Ferrie, Oswald and Cubans. Garrison becomes convinced that Oswald was an intelligence agent and a patsy. Eyewitnesses tell of shots from the Grassy Knoll and a stripper in Jack Ruby's club tells Garrison she met Oswald with Ruby. Ruby, in jail, begs Earl Warren to take him to Washington, where he can tell the whole story. As Garrison and Lou Ivon examine Dealy Plaza and conclude the killing was an ambush, flashbacks show us a fake Oswald attracting attention in Dallas and someone mocking up the famous backyard photo using someone else's body and Oswald's head. Meanwhile, the Vietnam War continues to escalate. Based on a tip that he is Bertrand, Garrison interviews businessman Clay Shaw, missing Easter lunch with his family. Next day, Garrison's investigation has been leaked to an hysterical press and the government announces Shaw is innocent. Ferrie calls in panic saying there is a contract on him. The next day he is dead, apparently of an heart attack, leaving two suicide notes. The FBI contacts Bill Broussard, saying Castro had JFK killed and, if Garrison persists, the truth could cause a war. In Washington, Garrison meets Colonel X who describes the assassination as a military coup organised by his superior, General Y, supported by the military manu-facturing business, because Kennedy wanted to end the cold war and pull US troops out of Vietnam. He tells Garrison truth is on his side. Garrison arrests Clay Shaw. He becomes the target of corruption investigations, his offices are bugged, his children threatened and his marriage disintegrates. Despite a lack of cooperation from authorities, the investigation persists and the conspiracy becomes more involved. Broussard refuses to accept such things and quits. Garrison won't call some key witnesses because their lives may be endangered. Robert Kennedy is shot. Garrison's wife returns. In court, Garrison details the conspiracy but loses a key point when testimony that Shaw acknowledged using the Bertrand alias is ruled inadmissible. He plays the Zapruder film for the jury, showing JFK's head being thrown backwards by the killing shot from the front. The jury finds Shaw innocent, saying they believed in the conspiracy but Shaw hadn't been proven part of it. End titles reveal Richard Helms of the CIA admitted Shaw was a CIA contact agent, Shaw's death, Garrison's reelection, the costs of the Vietnam war, the findings of the 1979 House Assassination Committee that a con-spiracy was probable, and, as a result of the controversy over this film, the setting up of a Congressional Committee to release many crucial docu-ments.

*Background:* The eerie thing about the media response to *JFK,* which we've detailed previously, is the way it echoes the response to Garrison's own investigation, with Stone taking over the Garrison rôle. Stone, of course, doesn't 'solve' the assassination, nor should he have to. What his film does, with great technical aplomb, is present the confusing swirl of possibilities and the relative certainty that the simple truth presented to the public has little likelihood of being accurate. Richardson commented that they tried to intercut formats and stocks to create a *Rashomon* effect in which various versions of the same story were all seen to have elements of truth.

As an exercise in combining a film story with a pseudo-documentary style reconstruction, *JFK* makes a complex subject understandable and entertaining; it would probably be more so had Stone not expanded the con-spiracy to include the Fletcher Prouty (the real Colonel X) theories as well. Still, Sutherland's Colonel X scenes play particularly well for such straight-forward exposition. They do, however, upset the film's balance because they are followed quickly by Garrison's own exposition in the courtroom.

For dramatic purposes, not because he has to 'solve' the crime, Garrison's theories need to be dovetailed with X's, which they don't always do. And after Sutherland's bravura delivery of his story, Costner's heavy-fisted approach, conveying Garrison's deep sense of offence that these crimes have happened, falls flat, though the Zapruder footage itself adds all the dramatic impact anyone could need.

As usual, Stone's real drama is one obsessed man's quest for enlightenment. Garrison is a crusader like James Stewart in *Call Northside 555* (the Stewart analogy is stretched further as Garrison's speech looks more and more like Stewart's filibuster in *Mr Smith Goes To Washington*) but Costner is unable to convey Stewart's underlying mania. Were Garrison's figure as conflicted as Stewart's, the film might well be more interesting but less successful, partly because Costner might not pull it off and partly because the story needs to be seen from Garrison's perspective, a point lost on most critics.

Stone was so taken with Garrison's *On The Trail Of The Assassins* he paid $250,000 for the film rights and enlisted the book's editor, Zachary Sklar, to work on the screenplay. Interestingly, Garrison had authored a previous book about the assassination, called *A Heritage Of Stone* (Putnam, 1970, in paperback from Berkeley Medallion, 1975—both editions disappeared quickly and are quite rare).

*Kramer vs. Kramer: JFK* is the film which, on the surface, most resembles a Stanley Kramer epic, particularly in the precise casting of even small parts. Many of the actors brought special resonance to their parts. Ed Asner, a public critic of US policy in Central America first drawn to Stone by *Salvador,* was cast against type as right-winger Guy Bannister. Jack Lemmon, America's conscience in *Missing, The China Syndrome* and *Save The Tiger,* added believability as Jack Martin as did Walter Matthau as the doubting Senator Long. John Candy revels in the part of the jive-talking lawyer Dean Andrews and Kevin Bacon takes scarcely less delight in playing the composite witness Willie O'Keefe. It is the conspirators, however, Tommy Lee Jones as Clay Shaw, Joe Pesci as David Ferrie and the almost silent Gary Oldman as Oswald who steal the show. Jay Sanders, Michael Rooker, Laurie Metcalf and Wayne Knight (whose character Numa, probably is echoed by the naming of his character Newman on the TV series *Seinfeld)* have the thankless task of bouncing off Costner.

*An Exercise In Genre:* Rather than see *JFK* as a historical documentary, which drove its critics mad, look at it as a detective story where Costner and Co. assemble the suspects, at least on film, before Costner gets to explain the plot to the jury and to us. It's pure Agatha Christie. When Colonel X does the same to Garrison you half expect him to say 'elementary, my dear Garrison' each time Costner expresses his amazement.

*The Thumper:* You are the jury! You decide! Kevin Costner is lecturing each and every one of you…do you get it? Do you? Backwards and to the left, backwards and to the left…

*The Verdict:* I find the first two thirds of *JFK* spellbinding, the last third didactic. The final scenes are the kind of exposition that usually get cut out of detective movies but the film remains endlessly watchable. Call that an riddle wrapped in an enigma inside a paradox. 5/5

## Nixon (1995)

*Cast:* Anthony Hopkins (Nixon), Joan Allen (Pat Nixon), James Woods (Bob Haldeman), J T Walsh (John Ehrlichman), Powers Boothe (Al Haig), Ed Harris (E Howard Hunt), Bob Hoskins (J Edgar Hoover), E G Marshall (John Mitchell), Madeleine Kahn (Martha Mitchell), Paul Sorvino (Henry Kissinger), David Hyde Pierce (John Dean), David Paymer (Ron Ziegler), Dan Hedaya (Trini Cardoza), Saul Rubinek (Herb Klein), Tony Plana (Manolo), Mary Steenburgen (Hannah Nixon), Tom Bower (Frank Nixon), David Barry Grey (Teenaged Nixon), Julie Condra Douglas (Young Pat), Tony Goldwyn (Teenaged Harold), Fyvush Finkel (Murray Chotiner), Larry Hagman ('Jack Jones'), Ed Herrmann (Nelson Rockefeller), Brian Bedford (Clyde Tolson), Tony LoBianco (Johnny Roselli), George Plimpton (President's Lawyer), Joanna Going (Student at Lincoln Memorial), Annabeth Gish (Julie Nixon), Marley Shelton (Tricia Nixon), John Diehl (Gordon Liddy), Sean Stone (Young Nixon), Joshua Preston (Young Arthur), Mikey Stone (Young Edward), John Bedford Lloyd (Cuban with Jack Jones), Donna Dixon (Mo Dean).

*Crew:* Producers: Clayton Townsend, Stone, Andrew G Vajna (Illusion Entertainment/Cinergi); Executive In Charge of Production: Tova Laiter; Co-Producers: Eric Hamburg, Dan Halstead; Associate Producer: Richard Rutkowski; Screenplay: Stephen J Rivele, Christopher Wilkinson, Stone; Photography: Robert Richardson; Time-Lapse Photography: Wayne D Goldwyn; Camera/Steadicam Operator: David Emmerichs; Editors: Brian Berdan, Hank Corwin; Production Design: Victor Kempster; Music: John Williams.

*Story:* The Watergate burglars are caught during the 1972 Presidential campaign. In 1973, at the White House, President Nixon has to deal with the first demands of the burglars in exchange for their silence. We learn Nixon's history in flashbacks which are intercut with the growing scandal of the Watergate cover-up. His personal life: born in California, his father is an unsuccessful farmer and shopkeeper, his mother a devout Quaker. Two of his brothers die of tuberculosis, one very young and the other, his idolised older brother Harold, when he is in high school; the death provides him with the wherewithal to go to college. At Whittier he spends four years on the bench of the football team, a 'tackling dummy' with no aptitude for the game. When he meets his future wife Pat it is love at first sight; he even drives her on her dates with other boys. He wins election to Congress after the War, running a red-baiting campaign against the incumbent and uses similar tactics to win another election. His rôle in the HUAC prosecution of Alger Hiss makes him a national name. He is elected Eisenhower's Vice President and survives a funding scandal by making the 'Checkers' speech, in which he insists his daughters will keep the puppy given them by his supporters. In 1960 he loses the presidential campaign to John Kennedy, whom he considered a friend from their days in Congress; Kennedy ambushes him with classified information in their debates and steals the election with voting fraud in Chicago (where his father has mob ties) and Texas (where his running mate is Lyndon Johnson). Nixon loses the 1962 California gubernatorial election and receives an ultimatum from Pat to quit politics. He tells the press "you won't have Nixon to kick around any more." In Dallas, the day before the Kennedy assassination, he is approached by Texas oilmen and Cubans to run for president but tells them Kennedy's re-election is a sure thing. In 1968, Johnson announces he will not run. Nixon returns to politics and the assassinations of Bobby Kennedy and George Wallace open the way for his victory. In the White House, Nixon continues the Vietnam war while trying to negotiate 'peace with honour', an exercise which gains added cynicism from the advise of Henry Kissinger. He establishes links with the Soviet Union and China but the footprints of Watergate continue to haunt him, most importantly the link to E Howard Hunt, who could open up what Nixon calls "the whole Bay of Pigs thing," a coded reference to the Kennedy assassination. As the pressure mounts, his drinking intensifies and he isolates himself from his wife. One by one, Nixon's aides are sacrificed to protect him until, finally, the existence of the White House tape recordings—and the 18½-minute gap in a crucial recording—make resignation his only option. In a coda, we see Bill Clinton eulogising Nixon at his funeral and then see his resignation speech as the closing credits roll.

*Background: Nixon* could be viewed as the other side of *JFK*, a detailed examination of a man in politics rather than an event. In fact, it sets up Nixon and Kennedy as yin and yang, a reflection of their actual closeness when they first came to Washington in the same year. Nixon's sense of betrayal when Kennedy 'cheats' in their debates is moving.

Audiences and critics were surprised by Stone's sympathy to Nixon the man and his appreciation of Nixon the diplomat. They were more surprised by his exposure of some of the negative sides of JFK, whom he had been accused of hero-worshipping. Criticisms of his portrayal of Nixon as a drunk have since been invalidated by revelation of the extent of his dependence on drink and prescription drugs.

As in *JFK*, the more you know, the more you will recognise: under the guidance of Murray Chotiner, Nixon virtually invented post-war negative campaigning, but it's hard to appreciate the resonance of those scenes from their necessarily brief introduction. The furore over *JFK* did not make Stone shy away from further conspiracy. Nixon is shown to be the knowing beneficiary, if not involved, in plots which resulted in the assassinations of the Kennedy brothers and the shooting of George Wallace. The whole "Bay of Pigs thing" is the centre of the conspiracy, a fact which would have been emphasised more by deleted scenes showing Nixon and the CIA's Richard Helms (played by Sam Waterston) playing blackmail games with each other.

Lost in the mix is the Howard Hughes connection, which would have been too much but might have provided valuable glue. Hughes' aide Robert Maheu, a link between the CIA and The Mafia, worked with Vice-President Nixon against Aristotle Onassis' moves into Saudi oil, funnelled Hughes' money to Nixon's campaigns via Bebe Rebozo (the Trini character played by Dan Hedaya) and loaned money to Nixon's brother Donald. Many people believed the Watergate burglary was intended to spy on Democratic Party chairman Larry O'Brien's own links with Hughes.

The film is actually stronger for its focus on Nixon the man rather than Nixon the conspirator. Nixon has been the most analysed of American leaders; studies of him virtually invented the genre of 'psycho-biography' in the early 1970s (the best is probably Gary Wills' *Nixon Agonistes*) and Stone is acutely aware of Nixon's place in the American psyche: the film begins with the Watergate burglars, who are supposed to be disguised as salesmen at a conference in case they are caught, being shown a Fifties sales-training film which is driving home the importance of looking your subject in the eye when making the sale. This, of course, will be the most patently false of Nixon's attempts at honest gesture, even more so than the forced smile which is at the heart of Anthony Hopkins' brilliant performance.

Hopkins doesn't try to imitate Nixon as much as enter into his physical space; his recreation of the man's tortured gestures, his forced smiles and eternal discomfort remind us that, just as Hopkins is playing Nixon, Nixon was playing 'Nixon' too, an idea reinforced by his constant references to himself in the third person which enables him to deliver his own thumper without even resorting to voice-over. Hopkins also draws on *Richard III*, surely Stone's favourite bit of the Bard, to add resonance to Nixon's sense of being physically ill-favoured, politically suspect but somehow still appealing to many.

*How Much Is Enough:* Nixon is probably Stone's most sympathetic character, certainly the first one we're drawn to pity since that other Richard III, Tony Montana. And it's interesting to see *Nixon* as a sort of political remake of *Scarface*. Nixon doesn't actually kill Kennedy but the king has to die before he can take over and then the lure of power proves as consuming to Nixon as coke did to Montana. And besides, the secrets within each character lurk in Cuba, don't they?

*Exploitation:* The film begins as a horror movie, with the White House and its menacing gates standing out in a storm and Alexander Haig, a creature of darkness, moving into Nixon's coffin-like room. Nixon, of course, is the prince of darkness whose ability to rise from the dead is illustrated more than once in the film (not just from childhood illness but from a pounding on the football field and his celebrated political comebacks). The film continues along those lines, with Paul Sorvino's Henry Kissinger, the most heavily made-up rôle in the film, coming to resemble a duplicitous Frankenstein's monster. Sadly, the make-up detracts from Sorvino's performance just as the film is let down somewhat by the Madame Tussaud's quality of Nixon's meetings with Mao and Brezhnev, a testament to the difficulties of trying to create, rather than suggest, lookalikes.

The opening also reminds us of *Citizen Kane* and as it takes us back into Nixon's childhood it will remind us, like Kane did, about the way the child's cold upbringing is reflected in the man. Nixon in the White House is Kane in Xanadu, with Woods and Walsh his Joseph Cotten. Recall, too, the earlier comparisons with Stone and Welles' own childhoods.

*Bit Parts:* Alex Butterfield, the man who made the Watergate tapes, plays a White House aide, as does former CIA officer and long-time critic John Stockwell. Producer Clayton Townsend is the floor manager when Nixon gives a TV speech.

*The Thumper:* They're lining up to thump you in this one. Joanna Going's impassioned student: "It's not you, it's the system!" ranks with Costner's wide-eyed "They killed him because he wanted to change things" as the most vacuous of Stone's political statements. Howard Hunt says, "You're going to learn he's the darkness." Pat cries "When do the rest of us start paying off your debts?" Sorvino's Kissinger comes closest when he says, "Can you imagine what this man would have been if he'd ever been loved? He had greatness in him." But the winner goes to the old trickster himself for the memorable aside to JFK's portrait, "When they look at you they see what they want to be. When they look at me they see what they are."

*The Verdict:* For all the thumpery this is an impressive historical film which holds up, though the power of Hopkins' performance dissipates as one becomes more familiar with it. Still, Hopkins and Allen shine, as do many of the cast, and Stone's psycho-biography, with its restrained hints at conspiracy, is engrossing. Of all Stone's characters, Nixon is probably the most sympathetic. 4/5

# 10: The Nineties Trilogy

In his three most recent films, Stone has appeared to be less searching for a cause than revisiting film itself, as if he had acquired a new influence: the Coen Brothers. What they have in common is a sense of coming at you from a media studies viewpoint, most obviously in *Natural Born Killers*. If many of the Coens films can be seen as essays on popular culture—*O Brother, Where Art Thou* examines folk music as American myth as surely as *Barton Fink* updates Nathanael West, or *Miller's Crossing* and *Blood Simple* revisit classic Hammett noir, and *The Man Who Wasn't There* lets Forties James M Cain meet Fifties SF—*Natural Born Killers* is an essay in TV and American violence…a *Raising Arizona* of violence. *U Turn* is an essay on the popularity of neo-noir style over film substance, set in an another Arizona which frames the film in irony. Even *Any Given Sunday* is a lament for the days when pro football was a game free of the pervasive influence of television and its money.

For most of his career, Stone had been ahead of the trends. *Salvador* and *JFK* made things happen in the real world and were prescient in the underlying truths they revealed. *Wall Street* was released at the point of a huge market crash which had people in a mood to reconsider, if only briefly, their devotion to 'market forces'. *Talk Radio* was still ahead of the real boom in 'shock jocks'. *Platoon* could be seen as the first film making it OK to revisit war as a potentially heroic undertaking.

This trilogy seems to be repsponding to events, and Stone began to revisit his own films as well. *Natural Born Killers* was *Scarface* meets *Talk Radio*. *U Turn*'s Bobby Cooper is Jim Garrison without the moral backbone. And *Any Given Sunday* puts Conan into a football stadium in Miami.

If Stone appeared more reactive in the late Nineties, he also seemed to be actively pursuing humour. *Natural Born Killers* is best viewed as black comedy like, say, Alex Cox's *Sid And Nancy*, whose lead couple are similarly lost in their own strange rules of love, enacting a bizarre version of a sitcom marriage. It might also be significant that it is around this time that Stone's marriage to Elizabeth Cox finally ended. Keeping marriages together is a major theme in *Nixon* and *Heaven And Earth* as well as *Natural Born Killers* and *U Turn*.

The early Nineties appeared to be a trying time for Stone personally. His second son, Michael, was born in 1991 but his marriage was already faltering. The break-up was precipitated when Elizabeth read Stone's diaries from his production trip to Thailand for *Heaven And Earth*. He also continued his spiritual quest through drugs. He and Rutkowski travelled to Brazil to experience ayahuasca shortly after finishing *JFK*. While working on *Heaven And Earth* he nearly died after overdosing on amino acids. It was soon after that he began to pursue his interest in Buddhism.

If, after that turnaround, *Nixon* was his most gentle film, *U Turn* is his most self-consciously funny film. But if the prevailing wind in the Nineties was ironic, self-referential humour, Stone's films remained more serious than most, and almost irony-free, as best illustrated by the depths he added to a Quentin Tarantino screenplay to produce yet another major controversy.

## Natural Born Killers (1994)

*Cast:* Woody Harrelson (Mickey Knox), Juliette Lewis (Mallory Knox), Robert Downey, Jr. (Wayne Gale), Tommy Lee Jones (Dwight McClusky), Tom Sizemore (Jack Scagnetti), Rodney Dangerfield (Mallory's Dad), Russell Means (Old Indian), Steven Wright (Dr Reingold), Joe Grisafi (Duncan Homolka), Pruitt Taylor Vince (Kavanaugh), Everett Quinton (Wurlitzer), Balthazar Getty (Gas Station Attendant), Lorraine Ferris (Pinky), Terrylene (Julie the Producer), Corinna Laszlo (Emily the Hostage), Melinda Renna (Antonia Chavez), Saomi Nakamura (Japanese Reporter), Jeremiah Bitsui (Young Indian), Dale Dye (Dale Wrigley), Glen Chin (Druggist), Carol-Renee Modrall (Cook), Richard Lineback (Sonny), Lanny Flaherty (Earl), O-Lan Jones (Mabel), Ed White (Pinball Cowboy), Edie McClurg (Mallory's Mom), Sean Stone (Kevin).

*Crew:* Executive Producers: Arnon Milchan, Thom Mount; Producers: Jane Hamsher, Don Murphy, Clayton Townsend (Warner Bros./Regency/Alcor/JD/Ixtlan); Co-Producer: Rand Vossler; Screenplay: David Veloz, Richard Rutkowski, Stone; Story: Quentin Tarantino; Photography: Robert Richardson; Editors: Hank Corwin, Brian Berdan; Production Design: Victor Kempster; Executive Music Producer: Budd Carr; Music Producer: Trent Reznor; Second Unit Director: Philip Pfeiffer.

*Story:* In a diner Mickey and Mallory kill rednecks who come on to her, then kill everyone else leaving only one witness. As they embark on a murder spree, we flash back to their first meeting and Mallory's abused childhood, presented like a *Married With Children* sitcom complete with Rodney Dangerfield as the father. Mickey arrives delivering meat; they kill her parents, sparing her brother, and leave, 'marrying' in a blood brother-type ceremony high above a gorge. As the spree continues, they become celebrity subjects of the TV show *American Maniacs*, hosted by Australian tabloid journalist Wayne Gale. They are also being pursued by celebrity author/cop Jack Scagnetti, a specialist in serial killers. Scagnetti hires a hooker who resembles Mallory and strangles her. When Mickey's taste in hostages proves to have sexual overtones and he suggests a threesome, Mallory leaves and seduces a gas station attendant, killing him when his clumsy sexual abilities bring her back to thoughts of Mickey. Reunited, Mallory gets them lost in the desert; out of gas and on foot, they encounter an old Indian shaman surrounded by snakes. In a drug-induced trance, Mickey shoots the Indian. Mallory is bitten by snakes. Killing a drugstore clerk who has sounded the alarm, they are captured by Scagnetti.

A year later, Warden McClusky summons Scagnetti to the prison where Mickey and Mallory are held, setting up a plan whereby he will murder the two who have become a risk to the prison population. Meanwhile, Gale has arranged to do a live interview with Mickey to be shown immediately after the Super Bowl. Mickey's description of himself as a "natural born killer" sets off a riot. In the confusion, Mickey disarms a guard, takes Gale hostage and frees Mallory, who has fought off a rape attempt by Scagnetti but is being beaten by guards. Gale, whose wife has discovered his affair, joins the two in killing guards—he ditches his wife by phone only to be dumped by his girlfriend. They escape and the riot consumes the warden. Mickey and Mallory turn Gale's camera on him and record their killing him. The final scenes show Mickey and Mallory living in a mobile home, as if beginning a new sitcom.

*Background:* It's hard to understand now why *Natural Born Killers* was greeted with such a furore, partly because its violent nihilism seems relatively tame only a few years later, but mostly because it plays like an essay into the effects of violence in mass media—and the resultant dumbing down of America—and makes its points with a lack of subtlety which, as ever, implicates Stone as having just as little faith in his audience as do the cynics who run network television. As ever, Stone exhibits his vicarious sort of fascination with TV, with Wayne Gale an unredeemable version of Pauline Axelrod crossed with Barry Champlain.

The original script of *Natural Born Killers* was part of Quentin Tarantino and Roger Avary's *The End Of The Road*, another part of which became *True Romance* and bits of which show up in both *Reservoir Dogs* and *Pulp Fiction*. Tarantino's *Natural Born Killers* is a sort of ironic *Gun Crazy* with more than a nod to *Badlands*. Its rights were owned by a young producing team, Don Murphy and Jane Hamsher, and once Stone had bought the script he had them hire a friend of theirs, David Veloz, to rewrite it, adding the sitcom background of Mickey and Mallory's relationship. When Stone came to the film and rewrote it again (with sidekick Richard Rutkowski), their changes infuriated Tarantino, whose efforts to stop the production and distance himself from it are detailed in Hamsher's piss and tell memoir. Stone and Rutkowski added the Indian shaman in the desert ("there's always an Indian in my films!") and the Wayne Gale sub-plot, Veloz the sitcom scene detailing Mallory's backstory, turning the focus to media satire—*Badlands* meets *Network*.

*The Thumper:* In case you miss the point, Mickey explains all in his interview with Wayne Gale (Gale: a breath of fresh wind?).

*Verdict:* When Mallory cries "This is sooo bad!" there is a strong temptation to agree. If you want to send a message, call Western Union not MTV. Even viewed as black comedy the satire is heavy-handed. The over-the-top nature of the performances will make this a cult classic in another 15 years or so, but for now, 3/5.

## U Turn (1997)

*Cast:* Sean Penn (Bobby Cooper), Jennifer Lopez (Grace McKenna), Nick Nolte (Jake McKenna), Powers Boothe (Sheriff Potter), Billy Bob Thornton (Darrell), Jon Voight (Blind Indian), Clare Danes (Jenny), Joaquin Phoenix (Toby N Tucker), Julie Hagerty (Flo), Abraham Benrubi, Richard Rutkowski (Robbers), Laurie Metcalf (Bus Clerk), Liv Tyler (Girl in Station), Sean Stone (Boy in Store), Bo Hopkins, Brent Biscoe (Guys in Diner).

*Crew:* Producers: Dan Halstead, Clayton Townsend (Phoenix/Illusion Entertainment); Screenplay: John Ridley, based on his novel *Stray Dogs;* Photography: Robert Richardson; Editors: Hank Corwin, Thomas Nordberg; Production Design: Victor Kempster; Music: Ennio Morricone; Second Unit Photography: Jerry Callaway; Time-Lapse Photography: William Goldwyn; Stunt Coordinator: Tierre Turner.

*Story:* Bobby Cooper is heading to Las Vegas to pay a debt to bookies who have already cut off two of his fingers. His car overheats and he stops in Superior, Arizona, to get it fixed. Told by mechanic Darrell the repair to the rare car will take time, Bobby takes his bag full of money into town. He goes home with Grace McKenna to help her hang curtains; her husband Jake catches them kissing, punches Bobby, but later offers him a ride as he walks back to town. He suggests that Bobby kill his wife in return for a cut of her insurance.

When a bodega owner kills two robbers with a shotgun, Bobby's bag of money is shot to ribbons. He gives the woman cash for her silence and now doesn't have the $150 Darrell wants for the repairs. In the local diner, teen-aged Jenny comes on to him and her boyfriend Toby (TNT) tries to start a fight. Bobby goes to McKenna and agrees to kill Grace, but when he takes her to a cliff he can't do it; as they make love (with Grace stopping him before climax) she tells him that was where her mother died, an apparent suicide. She suggests they kill Jake and steal the money he keeps in a safe under the floor; he wears the safe's key around his neck. Still preferring to get out of town, Bobby discovers the fee for his car is up to $200 and Darrell has a sign prepared to sell the car for $16,000.

Bobby convinces a clerk to take less than full fare for a ticket out of town but is ambushed by TNT, who eats the ticket before Bobby beats him up. Bobby now agrees to kill Jake; Grace will leave the door open for him. Jake corners him (using Bobby's gun which Darrell sold him) and Bobby agrees to kill Grace instead. When Jake enters the bedroom, the 'dead' Bobby attacks him. Eventually Grace kills Jake with a tomahawk. With the money, Bobby gets his car back from Darrell. Leaving town with Jake's body in the trunk, Bobby and Grace are stopped by Sheriff Potter, Grace's lover who expected her to double-cross Bobby. Grace kills Potter and reveals Jake was actually her father as well as her husband and that he killed her mother. They dump the two bodies, but Bobby hits Grace to get his gun back. She then pushes him off the cliff, not knowing he has the car keys. He lures her down the cliff. She shoots him but he kills her. Returning to the car despite his wounds and a broken leg, the water hose blows again. We see Bobby and the others dead.

*Background:* Stone's take on the popular run of neo-noir features might, on the surface, be compared to *Red Rock West* or *The Hot Spot* for its reliance on the small-town setting and heat as a metaphor as well as the stock situations of film noir. Or to *Palmetto* or even *The Last Seduction* for its pleasure at the self-delusions of its bozo hero. Men with one-track minds and half-track brains are the staple of film noir and Penn has lots of fun filling this role here. So does Stone. The butt cam shot of JLo's booty as Penn helps her hang drapes is worthy of Polanski at his most drooling. Note the classic noir moment when Bobby interrupts Grace just as she starts to tell him that Darrell and Jake are in cahoots. If he'd only listened!

Noir should be a natural for Stone because its characters are generally obsessed and usually make the wrong choices because of those obsessions. But, as we see when Bobby chooses the fork in the road to head to Superior because it has a spot called Apache Leap, for Stone the noir framework is an opportunity to breathe a whole new spectrum of colour and foreshadowing, if not mysticism, into it. A genre which thrives on claustrophobia and interior pressure resists such opening up.

Bobby is Richard Boyle washed up with a gun in a small desert town. It's loaded with desert symbolism and Indian mysticism; there's even Jon Voight playing a begging Indian shaman (who may or may not be a Vietnam veteran) complete with a dead guide dog who comes back to life. Voight's character reveals the strengths and weaknesses of the film in a nutshell. On the one hand it's full of U-turns—nothing is what it seems to be and things that are one thing turn out to be another. Every helicopter shot of roads shows us forks, separating paths, lay-bys and other detours, reminding us that noir is really about choices and having the freedom to make them. On the other hand, the progress of the characters down those roads becomes endlessly repetitive and even the Mickey and Mallory pair of Jenny and TNT seem like they've wandered in from the Stone oeuvre, rather than grown up in this dump.

*Incest In The Southwest:* The revelation that Jake is literally Grace's father (assuming you believe her) gives an explanation to Nick Nolte's turn playing John Huston in *Chinatown.* Nolte and Powers Boothe make a strong pairing, as Walter Hill discovered in *Extreme Prejudice* where they also shared involvement with a Latina queen. John Sayles' *Lone Star* also brought incestuous themes into the American Southwest which must say something about what looking at cactus all day long does to you (note too the similarity of the cactus to Penn's three-fingered hand).

*The Farce Side:* This is by far Stone's (intentionally) funniest movie. It is loaded with great situations—like tough guy TNT being called home to his mother—and fine lines—the absolute best being Potter's plaintive "we were going to go to Milwaukee" as Grace heads for Hawaii with Bobby. There is also a brilliant turn by Billy Bob Thornton as mechanic Darrell, who spends every scene U-turning with Penn. In another fit of inspired casting, Stone finds the perfect role for Liv Tyler, drawing out every ounce of her acting ability in a silent bit part as a girl waiting behind Sean Penn in the bus station.

*The Thumper:* Blessedly, there isn't one, though the fireside chat with Jon Voight, who basically warns Penn about what happens to noir heroes, almost qualifies.

*The Verdict:* At times the quick cuts of Indian mysticism really intrude. Is it suggesting that noirish greed is the price we pay for driving the Indians off their land and losing touch with our spiritual halves? If so, we don't really need it because the film loads so much into its third act, making it a *Titus Andronicus* of noir, it really needs to get there quicker with less portent. Still, the performances are wonderful and the humour genuine. A solid 3/5. Cut down and paced more obsessively it would have been 4/5.

# Any Given Sunday (1999)

*Cast:* Al Pacino (Tony D'Amato), Cameron Diaz (Christina Pagniacci), Dennis Quaid (Cap Rooney), Jamie Foxx (Willie Beamen), L L Cool J (Julian Washington), James Woods (Dr Harvey Mandrake), Matthew Modine (Dr Ollie Powers), Ann-Margaret (Margaret Pagniacci), Charlton Heston (Commissioner), Jim Brown (Montezuma Monroe), Lawrence Taylor (Shark Lavay), Aaron Eckhart (Nick Crozier), John McGinley (Jack Rose), Bill Bellamy (Jimmy Sanderson), Lela Rochon (Vanessa), Lauren Holly (Cindy Rooney), Elizabeth Berkley (Mandy Murphy), Andrew Bryniarski (Madman Kelly), Duane Martin (Willie's Agent), Clifton Davis (Mayor), Pat O'Hara (Tyler Cherubini), Bjorn Nittmo (Kicker), Stone (Tug Kowalski), Luciano Armellino (Bartender).

*Crew:* Executive Producers: Richard Donner, Stone; Producers: Lauren Shuler Donner, Dan Halstead, Clayton Townsend (Warner Bros./Ixtlan/ Donner); Co-Producers: Eric Hamburg, Jonathan Krauss, Richard Rutkowski; Screenplay: John Logan, Stone; Story: Daniel Pyne, Logan; Photography: Salvatore Totino; Additional DP: Keith Smith; Editors: Tom Nordberg, Keith Salmon, Stuart Waks, Stuart Levy; Music: Robbie Robertson, Paul Kelly, Richard Horowitz; Production Designer: Victor Kempster; Second Unit Director & Stunt/Football Coordinator: Allan Graf; Second Unit DP: Chuck Cohen.

*Story:* The Miami Sharks lose their fourth game in a row, but third-string QB Willie Beamen plays well replacing injured star Cap Rooney. Team owner Christina Pagniacci informs coach Tony D'Amato that she intends to get rid of Rooney. Beamen's individual ability leads the Sharks to a victory and he becomes a star, but his attitude drives away his girlfriend, Vanessa. Willie's rivalry with Julian and his refusal to follow the coach's team-oriented game plan create problems; D'Amato becomes perceived as old-fashioned and unable to 'relate' to young players. Although the team wins and Willie takes credit for it, he has also caused a teammate to be injured and he begins to lose the respect of the teammates. Meanwhile, Dr Powers discovers Shark Lavay has a potentially fatal injury, but Christina insists he must play and Dr Mandrake bullies him into accepting the decision. D'Amato goes along when Lavay signs a waver. D'Amato also brings back Rooney and in the big play-off game against Dallas he scores before being injured. Beamen, humbled by the veteran, sticks to the coach's game plan and leads the team to victory. Lavay is carried off the field but is not killed. At a celebration for his retirement as coach, D'Amato announces he has signed to coach a new expansion team and that he has already signed Beamen as his quarterback.

*Background:* In case you missed the significance in *Natural Born Killers* of Wayne Gale's interview with Mickey and Mallory taking place immediately after the Super Bowl, you can think of *Any Given Sunday* as being Stone's return to that thought and taking it to its excessive conclusion. This film fits in perfectly as the third of Stone's Nineties trilogy because it is concerned primarily with the bread (as in money) and circuses (as in media) nature of America's National Football League, a point hammered home with the usual gladiatorial subtlety by showing *Ben Hur* on a television and casting Charlton Heston as the league commissioner. The Roman analogy is a far from new one—Don DeLillo drew it specifically to Vietnam in his 1972 novel *End Zone*—nor is the comparison between football and war: in the 1920s, Grantland Rice likened a college backfield to the Four Horsemen of the Apocalypse.

Nor is the idea of television exploiting the violence. To an even greater extent than in *Natural Born Killers*, Stone undercuts his own perception by appearing to participate in, if not relish, the very same exploitation (not least by casting himself as a football TV commentator). Certainly the football scenes (some of which were cut, to the film's detriment, for the British release) are the strongest point of the film and among the best ever filmed.

As with many sports films, however, it's difficult for the film to match the original without exaggeration or excess and the eyeball rolling across the stadium turf can certainly be seen as one of Stone's most gratuitous moments of excess. Fiction does have its upside however: in the real NFL, a touchdown play as close as the film's decider would inevitably bring with it challenges and examination by the video referee, a delayed gratification not appropriate for film.

Of course the NFL wanted nothing to do with the film, which is why the teams are fictional (unlike the Arizona Cardinals, for example, in *Jerry Maguire*).

Structurally, the film is torn between its many conflicts with the result that few of them are given any real investigation. The one with the greatest dramatic potential, between doctors Woods and Modine (the film's most interesting actors), never really goes anywhere. This reflects the genesis of the screenplay which Stone had written years before, originally about an over-the-hill linebacker (basically the Lavay character). He then did a rewrite after reading a book about the reality of pro football's training rooms by Raiders' physio Rob Huizenga. The third version switched the focus to the quarterbacks and to the generational and racial issues.

The entire sub-plot of Cameron Diaz as a woman trying to make it in a man's world is awkward because she isn't really strong enough to do so and at times looks as if she doesn't really want to. Unless this is a level of irony so subtle as to be subliminal, it distracts from the other conflicts. Her mother, played by Ann-Margaret, appears to be another version of Stone's own mother, decorative and designed to party, not understanding why her daughter is concerned with the ugly world of men's business. Her attitude is, if this is what women really want why fight for equality in the world of pro football where the owners appear to be the same guys who sat around with 'Jack Jones' in *Nixon* plotting Kennedy's assassination?

*Behind The Camera:* This was Stone's first mature film made without Robert Richardson, who was shooting *Bringing Out The Dead* for Stone's teacher, Scorsese. Salvatore Totino, in his feature-film debut (his previous credits included the REM video 'What's The Frequency, Kenneth' and Radiohead's 'Fake Plastic Trees') provided the usual array of different formats and new technology (they made much use of Clairmont Camera's Image Shaker) to provide an intense, excessive look at the impact of the game. You'll see lots of influence of *Raging Bull* in his approach to getting violence onto film.

Totino was not a football fan but, after watching games with a cinematographer's eye, commented that football was "much slower than you think," something they took great pains to correct. They used a bungee camera, similar to the remote poolside camera used at swim meets, to provide a low tracking shot which emphasises the size and power of contact.

*You've Gotta Be A Football Hero:* Stone's own football 'career', which was over before he even started high school, was given great play in interviews, but this was his chance to indulge in a little hero worship. The sidelines are littered with pro football stars and legends: YA Tittle, Johnny Unitas, Dick Butkus, Pat Toomay and Warren Moon all play coaches; Joe Schmidt and then-current stars Terrell Owens, Irving Fryar and Ricky Watters make 'special appearances'; former Dallas coach Barry Switzer gets the sweet pleasure of playing an announcer and there are parts for lesser-known players like Pat O'Hara and Bjorn Nittmo. The bulk of the football was performed by players from the indoor Arena League. Among those originally cast, but who dropped out, were Puff Daddy, Ving Rhames and controversial NFL trash-talker Keyshawn Johnson.

Stone saved two rôles for special players. The first is Jim Brown as defensive coordinator Montezuma Monroe (yes, the nicknames are over the top). Brown, generally considered the greatest running back in football history, left his football career at its peak to go into films (starting with *The Dirty Dozen*) where he was inevitably less successful. Brown's other career, working with street gangs, also helped lend credibility to Stone's efforts with the players and in race relations. Brown was quick to point out in interviews the way Stone understood the reality of black perceptions, something evident in *Platoon* and that *Any Given Sunday* was, at heart, a black movie.

As Shark Lavay, Lawrence Taylor—the second special player—brought a layer of instant irony to the production. Taylor had been arrested for crack possession, giving his speech about drugs extra resonance. It also provided the impetus for his concussion sub-plot; if Taylor had been sentenced to prison during filming, the Lavay character would have been killed off.

Even the houses had authenticity. Miami Dolphin's quarterback Dan Marino's house was used for Cap's scenes at home. If you're going to look like a quarterback you've got to live like a quarterback.

*Look Mom, I'm On TV:* Stone yet again indulges his own fascination with the box, this time playing TV commentator Tug (those nicknames!) Kowalski (presumably an old-time star?). It's hard to avoid thinking of Stone actually being complicit in the very indulgences he condemns. But then indulgence is part of the Stone mystique.

*The Thumper:* Given that he is a football coach prone to motivational speeches, there are plenty from Pacino. But basically the address to the audience is narrated from a bar stool signifcantly, the same position .from which D'Amato will mis-interpet a whore's approach.

*The Verdict:* The longer version is actually more interesting, but the conflicts are just too many and resolved too quickly and the over-the-top moments pull it down. 2/5

# 11: Conclusion: Beyond Trilogies

Stone's next project has been elusive. He was originally supposed to be directing a film called *Beyond Borders* which he described as a nice love story between a wealthy philanthropist and a medical student doing relief work starring Angelina Jolie and Kevin Costner. Then it was Jolie and Ralph Fiennes. When the film finally went into production it starred Jolie and Clive Owen and was directed by Martin Campbell.

Stone had reportedly bought the film rights to *It Was Five Past Midnight*, the best-seller by French writer Dominique Lapierre (whose surname translates to 'the stone') about the Bhopal gas leak disaster which killed 22,000 people in India in 1984.

Stone's ex-wife has said she would like it if he made his long-contemplated film about the life of Alexander the Great, a project that would have obvious commercial promise following the success of *Gladiator*. At the time of writing, *Alexander* was in pre-production with Heath Ledger to star and due to start shooting in October 2002.

For all his typically Hollywood behaviour and for all his indulgence, Stone's seeking of power seems unblemished by the fear which is often found at power's heart. Blake's road to excess may lead to the palace of wisdom, but Blake never lived in Hollywood. Don't forget, producer Don Simpson, Hollywood's king of excess, died while reading a biography of Stone. Stone's own journey of personal excess often collides with the moral vision he seems unable to escape, and his successes and failures grow out of the conflict between those two elements. It is likely that whatever he directs in the future will be surprising, challenging and frustrating, but, above all else, entertaining.

# 12: Additional Credits

## Screenwriter

*Evita* (1996) directed by Alan Parker; screenplay by Oliver Stone and Alan Parker from the musical by Andrew Lloyd Weber and Tim Rice; produced by Alan Parker, Robert Stigwood and Andrew Vajna; starring Madonna, Antonio Banderas and Jonathan Pryce. In the late Eighties, Stone worked on a screenplay for the Lloyd Weber/Rice musical with Madonna envisioned as the star only to have her reject the idea because she didn't want to play a fascist. She changed her mind, however, once the character was explained to her, but demanded script approval and wanted to redo many of the songs herself. Others considered for the rôle included Paula Abdul but the project went ahead with Meryl Streep until she eventually dropped out over salary considerations. Stone moved on to *The Doors*, but his production team benefited from the work they had done in preparation for *Evita*. Stone made one more attempt at putting *Evita* together with Michelle Pfeiffer starring, but that too fell through. The film was eventually made, with Madonna back in the starring rôle with Alan Parker directing after rewriting Stone's screenplay. Stone has commented that he saw a lot of his mother in the character of Evita.

## Producer

*Reversal Of Fortune* (1990) (co-producer with Edward Pressman) directed by Barbet Schroeder; starring Jeremy Irons, Glenn Close, Ron Silver and Annabella Sciorra. Very much a Stone sort of story with Irons playing Von Bulow as if he'd internalised James Woods' entire oeuvre.

*Blue Steel* (1990) (co-producer with Pressman) directed by Kathryn Bigelow; starring Jamie Lee Curtis, Ron Silver, Clancy Brown, Elizabeth Pena and Louise Fletcher. One could also see Stone drawn to this chicks-with-guns story, though the finished product would let one down, as Curtis is forced to play a too stereotypical chick in distress.

*South Central* (1992) (co-producer) directed by Steve Anderson; starring Glenn Plummer, Byron Mimms, Lexie Bigham and Vincent Craig Dupree. Gang violence in LA? Oliver Stone? What an unusual idea.

*Indictment: The McMartin Trial* (1995) (co-producer for Ixtlan) directed by Mick Jackson; screenplay by Abby and Myra Mann; starring James Woods, Mercedes Ruehl, Lolita Davidovich, Sada Thompson, Henry Thomas and Shirley Knight. A made-for-TV movie produced by HBO, about the nursery owners tried for satanism in San Diego. Woods' manic lawyer learns compassion in a drawn-out version of *The Crucible* for the Nineties.

*The People Vs. Larry Flynt* (1996) (co-producer) directed by Milos Forman; starring Woody Harrelson, Courtney Love, Edward Norton and James Cromwell. This is so much like an Oliver Stone film it was billed as such when the National Portrait Gallery labelled some on-set photos for an exhibition! Larry Flynt is a typical Stone hero, pushing the limits and seeing his ideals of America shattered when his pushing brings the system down on him. Flynt's *Hustler* thus serves as an allegorical *JFK*. It's tough to find redemption through Courtney Love, though.

*Savior* (1998) (co-producer) directed by Pedrag Antonijevic; starring Nastassja Kinski, Pascal Rollin, Catlin Foster, Dennis Quaid and Stellan Skarsgård. The title of *Salvador* translated back into English, with a member of the Foreign Legion in Bosnia.

## Executive Producer

*Iron Maze* (1991) directed by Hiroaki Yoshida; starring Jeff Fahey, Bridget Fonda, J T Walsh, Horoaki Murakami and Gabriel Damon.

*Zebrahead* (1992) directed by Anthony Drazen; starring Michael Rapaport, Kevin Corrigan, Lois Bendler and Dan Ziskie (as Mr Cimino!).

*The Joy Luck Club* (1993) directed by Wayne Wang; starring Kieu Chinh, Tasi Chin, France Nuyen, Lisa Lu and Ming-Na Wen. Another natural, given Stone's *Heaven and Earth*, and in a more familiar context, more successful. Wayne Wang had been one of the most vocal attackers of *Year Of The Dragon*. As Stone says, "Things change—the first law of Buddhism."

*Wild Palms* (TV series, 6 hours, 1993) directors: Kathryn Bigelow, Keith Gordon, Peter Hewitt and Phil Joanou; starring James Belushi, Dana Delany, Robert Loggia, Kim Cattrall, Angie Dickinson, Bebe Neuwirth, Robert Morse, David Warner, Ernie Hudson, Nick Mancuso and Stone as Oliver Stone.

*New Age* (1994) directed by Michael Tolkin; starring Peter Weller and Judy Davis. A black comedy by the writer of *The Player* about Yuppies in mid-life crisis.

*Freeway* (1996) directed by Matthew Bright; starring Kiefer Sutherland, Reese Witherspoon, Bokeem Woodbine, Conchata Ferrell, Brooke Shields and Amanda Plummer.

*Killer: A Journal Of Murder* (1996) directed by Tim Metcalfe; starring James Woods, Harold Gould, Richard Council and Robert Sean Leonard.

***The Last Days Of Kennedy And King*** (TV documentary, 1998) directed by Vince DiPersio.

***The Corrupter*** (1999) directed by James Foley; starring Chow Yun Fat, Mark Wahlberg, Ric Young, Paul Ben-Victor and Jon Kit Lee.

***The Day Reagan Was Shot*** (TV movie, 2001) written & directed by Cyrus Nowrasteh; starring Richard Crenna (as Reagan) and Richard Dreyfuss.

## Interviewee

Stone also appears as the interviewee in *Oliver Stone On Alfred Hitchcock* (Turner Broadcasting with the British Film Institute, 1999) which tells us far more about Stone than Hitchcock. Stone says he is fascinated by the "appearance of respectability" in Hitchcock, how all his villains are "members of the establishment," and by Hitchcock's "love of political intrigue, the reality that lurks beneath the surface." It suggests Hitchcock might have been the perfect director for some of John le Carré, while Stone also thinks Hitch might've made *JFK*. With Melanie Griffith replacing Sissy Spacek, perhaps. Though it hardly seems to grow from a discussion of Hitchcock, Stone tells how receiving an "enormous amount of adverse criticism has "hardened me—helped me to go on."

## Unrealised Screenplays

The catalogue of Stone screenplays, treatments and projects is a fascinating one. This list is by no means complete and does not include the scripts already described in the text.

*Break* An early Seventies script in which a tortured poet goes off to Vietnam. Includes a seduction by one of his mother's friends and an encounter with his father's mistress.

*The Life And Times Of Duncan Davis* Based on Black Panther George Jackson.

*Horror Movie* A script about the making of a horror movie years ahead of *Scream*.

*The Demolished Man* Stone's screenplay based on Alfred Bester's classic SF novel was at one point going to be directed by Ted Kotcheff, well ahead of *Blade Runner*.

*Wilderness* An adaptation of Robert B Parker's novel lends itself to many of Stone's father/son thematics.

*Defiance* An early Eighties screenplay about Soviet dissidents.

*The Hillside Strangler* Around 1984 Stone was working with Floyd Mutrix on a screenplay about the LA serial killer, years ahead of *Silence Of The Lambs*.

*Contra* (aka *Company Man*) Two CIA men in Nicaragua. Around 1988, Stone liked the idea ('contra' means 'against') and wanted Paul Newman for the lead.

*Noriega* Stone has worked with a screenplay by Richard Wright on and off for years; at one point Al Pacino was rumoured to be starring.

*Tom Mix And Pancho Villa* Based on Clifford Irving's novel, a screenplay Stone was steering toward production shortly after his Oscar for *Platoon*.

*The Last Coyote* Stone was involved in attempt to make a film of Michael Connelly's novel, The Last Coyote, with Al Pacino as Hieronymous 'Harry' Bosch. Given that the book deals with Bosch reopening the investigation into the murder of his mother, a prostitute, it is an interesting choice which might have picked up resonance from Stone's own relationship with his mother.

# 13: Resources

## Video & DVD

This is a good time to be a Stone fan as virtually his entire oeuvre has been re-released in six and ten-movie VHS/DVD sets called 'The Oliver Stone Collection' which includes a career summary called *Oliver Stone's America*. Missing are *Seizure* and *The Hand,* both out of print, and the Hemdale titles, *Platoon* and *Salvador*, which were released in their own special editions by MGM in the summer of 2001. All the films in the set, except *U Turn* and *Talk Radio*, contain a director's commentary track. Four of them, *JFK*, *Nixon*, *The Doors* and *Any Given Sunday* include a bonus disc containing deleted scenes, 'making-of' documentaries and, with *Any Given Sunday*, screen tests and bloopers. *JFK* also contains an interview with Fletcher 'Colonel X' Prouty. The *Nixon* release includes the deleted scenes with Sam Waterston as Richard Helms. Both *JFK* and *Any Given Sunday* are billed as director's cuts.

Excerpts from Stone's student films can be found in *Oliver Stone: Inside/Out*, produced by Joel Sucher and Steven Fischler of Pacific Street Films for the BBC and Showtime in 1992. Both producers were classmates of Stone's at NYU. They are online at www.pacificstreetfilms.com.

## Internet

The official Oliver Stone site, www.oliverstone.com, is currently unavailable, not having moved when its former host went bust. There is an enthusiastic fan site, www.oscareworld.net/ostone, which offers information, opinion and feedback.

Audio and video coverage of Stone and Fletcher Prouty speaking at the National Press Club is available at www.astridmm.com/stone.

Tapes of Stone taking part in 'Hollywood and History', a 1992 debate organised by *Nation* magazine at New York's Town Hall, are available via www.thenation.com.

A Stone-debunking analysis of *JFK* called 'The Assassination Goes Hollywood' at http://macadams.posc.mu.edu/jfkmovie/htm seems even less dedicated to fact than the movie it criticises. Probe includes Jim DiEugenio's 'Oliver Stone vs. The Historical Establishment' at www.webcom.com/ctka/pr700-stone.html. Carl Oglesby's 'Who Killed JFK? The Media Whitewash' provides valuable background at www.ratical.com/ratville/JFK/JFKloot.html.

# Books

James Riordan's *Stone* (Hyperion Books, 1995) is well written and the most informative biography. Though it borders on the hagiographic, Stone's own sense of self-belief and fascination with the dark side of his image make him a remarkably honest interview. Chris Salewicz's *Oliver Stone Close Up: The Making Of His Movies* (Orion, 1997) is more telling in its analysis and includes the original *Variety* reviews of the films it considers. It was also done with Stone's cooperation, again warts and all. In an excellent profile, 'The Last Wild Man' (New Yorker, 8 August 1994), Stephen Schiff can barely believe his luck as he goes along for the ride with the newly-divorced Stone. David Thomson's *Biographical Dictionary Of Film* (Deutsch, 1994) remains an excellent starting point.

Frank Beaver's *Oliver Stone, Wakeup Cinema* (Twayne, 1994) is a more straightforward covering of the bases. *The Cinema of Oliver Stone* by Norman Kagan (Roundhouse, 1995) is relatively superficial, including long excerpts of dialogue from each film. Coming out just before *Natural Born Killers*, it assumed that the film would be a "satirical comedy" which, as noted, is probably right. *Oliver Stone's America: Dreaming The Myth Outward* by Susan Mackay-Kallis (Westview Press, 1996) is about as clear as its title. *Oliver Stone Interviews*, edited by Charles Silet (Mississippi University Press, 2001), is another in that valuable series, including at least five interviews I'd sought out separately. Also valuable is the Oliver Stone issue of *Creative Screenwriting* (Vol. 3 No. 2, Fall 1996) which includes three essays on Stone, another on historical films, an analysis of the screenplay of *Salvador* and an interview with David Veloz. George Hickenlooper's *Reel Conversations* (Citadel 1991) includes a good Stone interview.

The original screenplays of *Talk Radio* by Eric Bogosian (Faber & Faber, 1989) and *Natural Born Killers* by Quentin Tarantino (Faber & Faber, 1995) are both essential reading to show how Stone approached the raw material of each film.

Jane Hamsher's *Killer Instinct* (Broadway, 1996) is self-promoting, as you'd expect from a young producer, and it's hard to believe she 'saved' the screenplay of *Natural Born Killers* herself. She's actually more revealing—and funnier—about Tarantino than Stone, but her image of Stone as an emotional button-pushing pothead Buddhist Godard is compelling, especially when Stone tells her she "just wants to get fucked by greasy garage mechanic types," making you wonder exactly where Mallory's drives originate. Stone's own novel, *A Child's Night Dream* (St. Martin's, 1997), has obviously been rewritten from its earlier state but still reads like a cross between Thomas Wolfe and Céline.

It's fascinating and amazing that any film director could generate such academic and political debate as Stone has, even more so that he would remain involved in that debate. I can't see Frank Capra arguing politics with Walter Lippman after making *Mr Smith Goes To Washington*.

If you're interested in pursuing the issues around *JFK*, the place to start is the annotated screenplay, *JFK: The Book Of The Film* (Applause, 1992) which not only contains the original script with footnotes justifying its assumptions but also a full and balanced record of the debate over the film, notable largely for the figures, like George Will, who refused to let their published comments be reprinted. It enabled me to clear out many old clippings from my files. I doubt any film has ever generated a similar volume and range of criticsim, and it's an instructive and worthwhile read. The *JFK* issue of *Cineaste* (Vol. 19 No. 1, 1992) is almost as valuable. Editor Gary Crowdus has been Stone's favourite interviewer and has a firm grip on the political issues. It also includes interviews with scripter Zach Sklar and researcher Jane Rusconi and a number of illuminating essays.

My favourite of the one-volume compendia on the assassination is Anthony Summers' frequently updated and retitled *Conspiracy* (Gollancz, 1980, aka *The Kennedy Conspiracy* and *Not in Your Lifetime*). Jim Marrs' *Crossfire* (Pocket, 1993, originally published in 1988) remains in print. The most valuable recent book, benefiting from access to documents made available following the controversy sparked by *JFK*, is *Oswald Talked* by Ray and Mary LaFontaine (Pelican Press, 1996) which helps explain what Oswald may have thought he was doing when he was used as a patsy. Robert Groden was an adviser to Stone on the film (he's the projectionist for the showing of the Zapruder film in *JFK*'s courtroom scene) and his two picture volumes, *The Killing Of A President* (Viking, 1993) and *The Search For Lee Harvey Oswald* (Bloomsbury, 1995) are useful. The two sides of Jim Garrison are explored by Patricia Lambert's *False Witness* (M Evans, 1999) which is anti-Garrison and thus received most of the attention, and Bill Davy's pro-Garrison *Let Justice Be Done* (Jordan, 1999) which is more honest.

*Oliver Stone's USA: Film, History, And Controversy,* edited by Robert Toplin with commentary by Stone (Kansas University Press, 2000), includes historical debates on his films from leading journalists and historians as well as Stone's responses to them. The annotated screenplay of *Nixon* (edited by Eric Hamburg, Bloomsbury, 1996) is less immediate but features some interesting essays by people involved with the man, including a cynical memo on Ted Kennedy written by the right fork of Nixon's tongue, Pat Buchanan).

# Articles

Bauer, Eric, Interview, *Creative Screenwriting*, Fall 1996.

Biskind, Peter, 'Cutter's Way', *Premiere*, February 1990.

Breskin, David, Interview, *Rolling Stone*, 4 April 1991.

Cockburn, Alexander, 'Oliver Stone Takes Stock', *American Film*, December 1987.

Combs, Richard, 'Doors', *Sight & Sound*, July 1991.

Cooper, Marc, Interview, *Playboy*, February 1988.

Crowdus, Gary, 'Personal Struggles & Political Issues', *Cineaste* Vol. 16 No. 3, 1988.

Dutka, Elaine, 'What Would Happen', *Empire*, March 1990.

Floyd, Nigel, 'Radical Frames of Mind', *Monthly Film Bulletin*, January 1987.

Hibbin, Sally, 'Salvador', *Films & Filming*, January 1987.

Horton, Robert, 'Riders On The Storm', *Film Comment*, May/June 1991.

Konow, David, 'The World Is Yours', *Creative Screenwriting*, July/August 2001.

Leahy, James, 'Salvador', *Monthly Film Bulletin*, January 1987.

Lewinski, John Scott, 'Wealth With Honour', *Creative Screenwriting*, Fall 1996.

Manso, Peter, 'Stone's Throw', *Premiere*, January 2000.

McGilligan, Pat, 'Point Man', *Film Comment*, January/February 1987.

Pizzello, Chris, 'Smash-Mouth Football', *American Cinematographer*, January 2000.

Posner, Gerald, 'Garrison Guilty', *NY Times Magazine*, 6 August 1995, and letters contradicting Posner the following week.

Porton, Richard, 'Porn Again' (Milos Forman interview), *Cineaste*, January 1997.

Sammon, Paul, features on *Conan*, *Cinefantastique*, September 1981 and April 1982.

Scheer, Robert, 'Born On The Third Of July', *Premiere*, February 1990.

Smith, Sam, 'Why They Hate Oliver Stone', *Progressive Review*, February 1992.

Talbot, Stephen, 'Sixties Something', *Mother Jones*, March/April 1991.

Williams, David, 'Great Relationships', *American Cinematographer*, November 1998.

Wills, Gary, 'Dostoyevsky Behind A Camera', *Atlantic Monthly*, July 1997.

Wood, Robin, 'Hero/Anti-Hero', *Cine-Action*, Summer/Fall 1986

Wrathall, John, 'Greeks, Trojans, and Cubans', *Monthly Film Bulletin*, October 1989.

# The Essential Library: Best-Sellers

Build up your library with new titles every month

**Alfred Hitchcock** by Paul Duncan

More than 20 years after his death, Alfred Hitchcock is still a household name, most people in the Western world have seen at least one of his films, and he popularised the action movie format we see every week on the cinema screen. He was both a great artist and dynamite at the box office. This book examines the genius and enduring popularity of one of the most influential figures in the history of the cinema!

**Stanley Kubrick** by Paul Duncan

Kubrick's work, like all masterpieces, has a timeless quality. His vision is so complete, the detail so meticulous, that you believe you are in a three-dimensional space displayed on a two-dimensional screen. He was commercially successful because he embraced traditional genres like War (*Paths Of Glory*, *Full Metal Jacket*), Crime (*The Killing*), Science Fiction (*2001*), Horror (*The Shining*) and Love (*Barry Lyndon*). At the same time, he stretched the boundaries of film with controversial themes: underage sex (*Lolita*); ultra violence (*A Clockwork Orange*); and erotica (*Eyes Wide Shut*).

**Orson Welles** by Martin Fitzgerald

The popular myth is that after the artistic success of *Citizen Kane* it all went downhill for Orson Welles, that he was some kind of fallen genius. Yet, despite overwhelming odds, he went on to make great Films Noirs like *The Lady From Shanghai* and *Touch Of Evil*. He translated Shakespeare's work into films with heart and soul (*Othello*, *Chimes At Midnight*, *Macbeth*), and he gave voice to bitterness, regret and desperation in *The Magnificent Ambersons* and *The Trial*. Far from being down and out, Welles became one of the first cutting-edge independent film-makers.

**Woody Allen (Revised & Updated Edition)** by Martin Fitzgerald

Woody Allen: Neurotic. Jewish. Funny. Inept. Loser. A man with problems. Or so you would think from the characters he plays in his movies. But hold on. Allen has written and directed 30 films. He may be a funny man, but he is also one of the most serious American film-makers of his generation. This revised and updated edition includes *Sweet And Lowdown* and *Small Time Crooks*.

**Film Noir** by Paul Duncan

The laconic private eye, the corrupt cop, the heist that goes wrong, the femme fatale with the rich husband and the dim lover - these are the trademark characters of Film Noir. This book charts the progression of the Noir style as a vehicle for film-makers who wanted to record the darkness at the heart of American society as it emerged from World War to the Cold War. As well as an introduction explaining the origins of Film Noir, seven films are examined in detail and an exhaustive list of over 500 Films Noirs are listed.

# The Essential Library: Recent Releases

Build up your library with new titles every month

**Tim Burton** by Colin Odell & Michelle Le Blanc

Tim Burton makes films about outsiders on the periphery of society. His heroes are psychologically scarred, perpetually naive and childlike, misunderstood or unintentionally disruptive. They upset convential society and morality. Even his villains are rarely without merit - circumstance blurs the divide between moral fortitude and personal action. But most of all, his films have an aura of the fairytale, the fantastical and the magical.

**French New Wave** by Chris Wiegand

The directors of the French New Wave were the original film geeks - a collection of celluloid-crazed cinéphiles with a background in film criticism and a love for American auteurs. Having spent countless hours slumped in Parisian cinémathèques, they armed themselves with handheld cameras, rejected conventions, and successfully moved movies out of the studios and on to the streets at the end of the 1950s.

Borrowing liberally from the varied traditions of film noir, musicals and science fiction, they released a string of innovative and influential pictures, including the classics *Jules Et Jim* and *A Bout De Souffle*. By the mid-1960s, the likes of Jean-Luc Godard, François Truffaut, Claude Chabrol, Louis Malle, Eric Rohmer and Alain Resnais had changed the rules of film-making forever.

**Bollywood** by Ashok Banker

Bombay's prolific Hindi-language film industry is more than just a giant entertainment juggernaut for 1 billion-plus Indians worldwide. It's a part of Indian culture, language, fashion and lifestyle. It's also a great bundle of contradictions and contrasts, like India itself. Thrillers, horror, murder mysteries, courtroom dramas, Hong Kong-style action gunfests, romantic comedies, soap operas, mythological costume dramas... they're all blended with surprising skill into the musical boy-meets-girl formula of Bollywood. This vivid introduction to Bollywood, written by a Bollywood scriptwriter and media commentator, examines 50 major films in entertaining and intimate detail.

**Mike Hodges** by Mark Adams

Features an extensive interview with Mike Hodges. His first film, *Get Carter*, has achieved cult status (recently voted the best British film ever in *Hotdog* magazine) and continues to be the benchmark by which every British crime film is measured. His latest film, *Croupier*, was such a hit in the US that is was re-issued in the UK. His work includes crime drama (*Pulp*), science-fiction (*Flash Gordon* and *The Terminal Man*), comedy (*Morons From Outer Space*) and watchable oddities such as *A Prayer For The Dying* and *Black Rainbow*. Mike Hodges is one of the great maverick British filmmakers.

# The Essential Library: Currently Available

Film Directors:

| | | |
|---|---|---|
| Woody Allen (Revised) | Tim Burton | Ang Lee |
| Jane Campion* | John Carpenter | Steve Soderbergh |
| Jackie Chan | Joel & Ethan Coen | Clint Eastwood |
| David Cronenberg | Terry Gilliam* | Michael Mann |
| Alfred Hitchcock | Krzysztof Kieslowski* | Roman Polanski |
| Stanley Kubrick | Sergio Leone | Oliver Stone |
| David Lynch | Brian De Palma* | |
| Sam Peckinpah* | Ridley Scott | |
| Orson Welles | Billy Wilder | |
| Steven Spielberg | Mike Hodges | |

Film Genres:

| | | |
|---|---|---|
| Blaxploitation Films | Bollywood | French New Wave |
| Horror Films | Spaghetti Westerns | Vietnam War Films |
| Vampire Films* | Heroic Bloodshed* | |
| Slasher Movies | Film Noir | |

Film Subjects:

| | | |
|---|---|---|
| Laurel & Hardy | Marx Brothers | Animation |
| Steve McQueen* | Marilyn Monroe | The Oscars® |
| Filming On A Microbudget | Bruce Lee | Film Music |

TV:

Doctor Who

Literature:

| | | |
|---|---|---|
| Cyberpunk | Philip K Dick | The Beat Generation |
| Agatha Christie | Sherlock Holmes | Noir Fiction* |
| Terry Pratchett | Hitchhiker's Guide | Alan Moore |
| Stephen King | | |

Ideas:

| | | |
|---|---|---|
| Conspiracy Theories | Nietzsche | UFOs |
| Feminism | Freud & Psychoanalysis | Bisexuality |

History:

| | | |
|---|---|---|
| Alchemy & Alchemists | The Crusades | The Black Death |
| Jack The Ripper | The Rise Of New Labour | Ancient Greece |
| American Civil War | American Indian Wars | |

Miscellaneous:

| | | |
|---|---|---|
| The Madchester Scene | Stock Market Essentials | Beastie Boys |
| How To Succeed As A Sports Agent | | |

Available at all good bookstores or send a cheque (payable to 'Oldcastle Books') to: **Pocket Essentials (Dept OS), 18 Coleswood Rd, Harpenden, Herts, AL5 1EQ, UK**. £3.99 each (£2.99 if marked with an *) . For each book add 50p postage & packing in the UK and £1 elsewhere.